Endorsements

"*A book for anyone searching to understand why they are the way they are and how to heal and move forward in a healthy and empowering way. Dana's personal stories are beyond relatable, and she writes in a way that you feel you are having a 1:1 conversation with her. This book has ignited memories that I completely buried over the years and has given me a sense of understanding my behaviors, so that I can learn from them, let go and grow! Thank you Dana Sardano!*"
Tara G.

"*Dana's words flow like a conversation between trusted friends in this engaging and interactive psychological masterpiece. Her raw and painfully honest relatability provide a clear and methodical explanation of what makes each and every one of us tick and provides us with the tools we need to shed the ties that bind.*"
Ann Marie S.

"*This book is eye opening! Powerful! A must read if you want to transform your life!*"
Kimberley C.

D1470678

"*After reading Ten Recommandments for Personal Empowerment, I had experienced healing, personal growth, and truths that I had not been able to see or experience before picking up this insightful read. Thank you Dana Sardano for sharing your story, the steps that you have chosen to better yourself, and for offering your gained knowledge and wisdom to assist others with their own personal journeys of healing and personal growth. Connecting with your stories and applying your "how-to" approach to self-awareness has been the catalyst to my own healing journey. I am forever changed.*"

Laurie B.

"*Read this book! It takes you on a journey to being your best self. The guidance, insights and wisdom shared in this book are second to none. I found myself highlighting text at every turn.. Thank you Dana for writing this book. You are brilliant.*"

Lisa

"*Firstly, I adore Dana's writing style, and I found her life story fascinating! So impressive how she can connect all those dots, patterns, life lessons, limiting beliefs for herself and then articulate so well for others to understand. Having insight of her story really makes the concepts feel relevant and relatable. I couldn't put it down! I read it in two sittings.*"

Cristen G.

"*I absolutely loved the book. I couldn't put it down. This is the kind of book that you want to go back and re-read and do some journaling. This book definitely spoke to me and made me rethink and reevaluate my life. It motivated me to pursue what I want out of my life and to let go of those past relationships that broke my heart to pieces. Thank you for writing this book.*"
Sulay N.

"*This book is a DEFINITE read for those who are on a honest path of self-discovery and self-empowerment. Dana's raw and grounded story telling provokes deep contemplation of the un-healed experiences we've all had. Ten Recommandments goes even further, layer by layer, to help us grow from this new space of self-awareness into self-empowerment. Thank you for this Life-Changing book, Dana!*"
Wendy Bee

"*This book screams volumes for every walk of life. To the teenager that wants to feel empowered and learn early on, to the single parent who has dealt with life's bumpy journey, to the successful artist who just needs some clarification on life. It made me cry, to feel vulnerable, as if the book was meant exactly for me. Dana's book is a must read.*"
Miss Marie

"I received this book in a time of complete angst with the thoughts of 'there has to be more than this.' Since I've read this and applied this knowledge, I have been equipped to face challenges with new techniques and perspectives. Allow this book to help you recognize what's holding you back from your best way of being, and approach your fears in ways that promote growth and empowerment."

Mattie D.

"I LOVED this book. The author's personal story is so compelling, and I love how she uses it as an example of how she grew from where she was to where she is now. It's truly inspiring to realize that there are other people that have struggled through similar things growing up, how we can break free from the thought cycles we get stuck in and create new patterns that make us much better versions of ourselves. If you really want to grow, then this is a must read!"

Anonymous

"Dana Sardano's Ten Recommandments for Personal Empowerment is a must read for anyone looking to move forward with their life in a healthy and whole way. Her recommendments allow the reader to look at their past experiences with fresh eyes so they are better able to discern the necessary lessons while leaving the emotional attachment behind...where it

belongs. Even if you believe you have already "done the work" and put most of your "traumas" to rest, there is something here to be gleaned. As Dana points out, and as many of us have experienced, there is almost always another layer of the onion to be unraveled. Ten Recommandments assist the reader in healing those inner-most layers once and for all."
Michelle G.

"The insights that I have uncovered from not only reading this book but following the expertly laid out guidance and suggestions is beyond compare to any 'self-help' book that I've ever read. Ten Recs taught me how to be the best advocate for my personal empowerment and wellbeing and also that the answers lie within each of us. I don't need to seek external rituals and practices and therapies to achieve contentment! This is a total game-changer, but it's definitely not for wimps!"
Angela D.

Other Works by Dana Sardano

Beyond the Ten, Decoding the Woo Woo

Veda Finds Her Crown

Veda Finds Her Crown Cards for Chakra Empowerment
and Personal Development

Ten Recommandments Cards for
Personal Empowerment

Soul Traveler Cards for Empowerment
in Collaboration with Ann Marie Skordy

Ten Recommandments

for

Personal Empowerment

Written by

Dana Sardano

First printing in the U.S.A. in 2022 by

φ
Phenom
PUBLISHING

A DIVISION OF THE UNIQUELY U. GROUP LLC
NEW YORK, NEW YORK

Cover and Interior Artwork by Dana Sardano, Copyright © 2022
Cover and Interior Design by Angela DiMarco

Second Edition 2022

ISBN 979-8-9872105-1-2

Dedication

I would like to thank all the people that played a part in the creation of this book—both the unicorns that I hold dear as well as the ancillary players in my story. Regardless of your part being good, bad or ugly, I appreciate your contribution. My life is better for having known you. I truly hope you can say the same.

Last but not least, my Schmoopy, I would be lost without you. Once I got a glimpse of ME through the eyes of YOU, did my life truly begin. Here's to our vegetable world!

I love all of you.

Thank you and ubuntu!

Dana

Ten Recommandments for Personal Empowerment

Written by Dana Sardano

Table of Contents

Forward

I remember very well when Dana first wrote the *Ten Recommandments*. While in the throes of her and her family down for the count with Covid, she'd jot notes in her phone and then go back to sleep, rinse and repeat. One day, when she was feeling a bit better, Dana typed out all her little nugs and realized there were ten of them, and then she realized that she had quite a bit of insight to offer on each and thus, her book *Ten Recommandments for Personal Empowerment* was born.

Every time Dana wrote a chapter or a story within a chapter, she'd send it to me, her husband and some other close friends to read. Her hope was to receive feedback, but what actually happened was that because I was so ready for the guidance and her sage advice, my experience of having exponentially grown as a result of my reading her manuscript was all the evidence we both needed to understand that what Dana was spewing out was pure f-ing gold.

Dana's writing style is unlike any other that I've encountered in a book. Her personal stories are raw, vulnerable, (that Oxford comma is for you, Boo!) and authentic, allowing the reader to feel so deeply connected to her humanness. It's like she's a "grunge author" because her openness is similar to those songwriters of the 90's—but then she balances these heart-felt stories with profound guidance that is very sound and grounded, exhibiting evidence of her 25+ years as a career educator. I don't know anyone else that can so eloquently use expressions such as "entrenched in our emotions" and "twat punch" in the same paragraph, but she does so expertly with the balance of a tightrope walker.

For those of you who don't know, Dana is also a fine artist and gallery owner. After the manuscript was complete and in the publisher's hands for editing, I watched her create another masterpiece, her cover girl "Chloe"—a beautiful expression of a girl who has become fully empowered and now resides in Ubuntu Fish Gallery. It was such an honor to design this book cover—it was as if Chloe was cheering me on to live my newly empowered best life ever!

The first edition of this book was published by an indie publisher in the UK on April 30, 2022. Since then, Dana has written her follow-up book, *Beyond the Ten, Decoding the Woo Woo* (another book that's pure f-ing gold), became the Co-Founder, Chief Officer of Content + Curriculum, and my Consigliere of my company, FindUniquelyU.com, the co-host of our talk show "Cuddle Talk with Angela & Dana", and Co-Founder and Editor-in-Chief of our latest collaboration, Phenom Publishing.

This new edition of *Ten Recommandments for Personal Empowerment* includes a few new testimonials, some copy edits and formatting updates, and is released under our sparkly, new imprint. It only makes sense that *Ten Recs* be our flagship book because it truly inspires and empowers all aspiring authors to share their story and to also become a phenom.

Angela DiMarco
Founder/CEO, FindUniquelyU.com
Co-Founder/Chief Creative Officer, Phenom Publishing
Co-Host "Cuddle Talk with Angela & Dana"
Friend

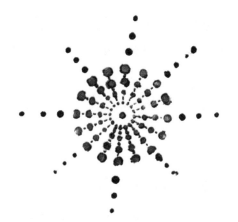

XVI

Everyone has a story.

I have a story.
You have a story
We ALL have a story.

As I see it, you have three choices:

Allow your story to define you.
Use it to excuse you.
Or, utilize it as a method to
empower you.

It's your life.
It's your story.
You have the power.
YOU choose.

After all, it's YOUR story!

XVIII

Prologue: This is my story.

Most of my life had been a struggle, and I had always felt very much alone. For most of my adult life, I had prided myself on being "an island", a singular being, the ONLY person to look out for my well-being. I took pride in my independence, my resilience, and my ability to bulldoze obstacles in any and all situations.

What I've learned through the process of self-exploration is that our personal empowerment is directly linked to our ability to look within and ultimately recognize that we are all interconnected and we are all essentially in this together. I learned that *I* didn't just suffer; we *all* suffer. Our humanness is based on suffering, and this suffering binds us and hopefully teaches us compassion for ourselves and others along the way.

What I also learned is, I and I alone am responsible for my own suffering, and when I begin taking the steps toward releasing that suffering, then I will truly feel empowered.

This book is intended to reveal how I taught myself to navigate life's opportunities to learn, grow, and overcome the more challenging obstacles with more grace and less discomfort than before. I eventually even embraced these opportunities, and I aim to offer some insight into how you could do the same.

My discovering and defining of any of the *Ten Recommandments for Personal Empowerment* cannot be linked to any one specific experience; rather, they are a compilation of insights that I have collected over the years that have appeared repeatedly through my own life story. Upon further reflection of each life experience, all arrows have consistently pointed to one, two, or several of these basic understandings, and when I began to utilize these understandings in my own life and change my beliefs and patterns was when my own life began to change direction.

To offer some context for the Ten Recommandents that lie ahead, the next few pages are a loose account of the life experiences that brought forth these insights.

Part I: My Belief Systems

In order to best understand some of my old belief

systems and patterns, I will briefly explain my family dynamic. I am the second child in an Italian family; the first born was my brother. Traditionally, in Italian families, the first-born son is revered and daughters, in general, not so much. Our family fit this profile.

Both of my parents were extremely attractive and charismatic but carried irrational belief systems and toxic behaviors and patterns of their own. For the sake of ease and the economy of words, and although nobody is ever just one thing, my mother's parenting style could be characterized as neglectful, at least with her daughter— with her son, it was more doting. My father's parenting style could be characterized as more abusive in comparison to my mother.

As an adult, of course, I understand that they didn't have the understanding of themselves nor the tools to parent in a healthy way, but as a child, my beliefs were shaped by my child brain's perspective. As an adult, I understand that my mother had abandonment, worthiness, and self-esteem issues from her own childhood, creating patterns driven by fear and lack of self-worth. Although it's difficult to comprehend, on some level, she was a little jealous of me because the spotlight that she desperately needed to feel worthy shifted to me when I was

3

born. My being a more energetic, aggressive, and sensitive child than my brother certainly didn't help the situation.

As an adult, I understand that my father, who had a very generous and sensitive nature, had incredible imbalances in his disposition that were driven by fear and his own feelings of unworthiness. He was extremely volatile and could "flip a table" in an instant.

My father followed all of the rules: He was well-educated, professionally employed, had a beautiful wife, a beautiful family, and a beautiful house in the suburbs. He followed all of the rules but chose a life that was extremely stressful—he was a hot shot executive in NYC with an arduous commute, had a wife that was emotionally distant, adhered to rules and societal conditioning that were not in alignment with his heart, and was unable to process his emotions in a healthy way—and of course, my being a more energetic, aggressive, and sensitive child (who in a lot of ways was just like him) certainly didn't help the situation.

As an adult, I understand both of my parents from a relatively objective and detached perspective. As a child, however, I walked away with many beliefs about myself that never quite served me.

- *I believed that I was unworthy of love and that I'd*

always have to work harder to be loved.

- *I believed that my needs did not matter.*
- *I believed that when I expressed my needs, I was "a beast" or "a monster" or "a one-way street".*
- *I believed the only way to express my displeasure was through fits of rage.*
- *I believed that I was loved less than my brother.*
- *I believed that problems were either attacked or ignored.*
- *I believed the only person that I could ever count on for anything was myself.*
- *I believed that life was hard, and I must fight to overcome obstacles to get my needs met.*

These beliefs about myself were the foundation for some pretty prominent patterns in my life, one of which (and probably the most prominent) was the pattern of relationships based on either abuse or neglect. My childhood experiences laid the foundation for many dysfunctional relationships in my life, most of all my relationship with myself.

I will save the lengthy version for a more comprehend-sive autobiography, but for context, by the time I was 12 years old, my parents were divorced. At 14 years old, I became estranged from my father. At 17 years old, I graduated high school, and at 18 years old, I went off to college in a completely different state over 1,200 miles away. There, I began to shift my unhealthy beliefs and patterns into high gear.

My unhealthy state of being was evident in my 20's but certainly not as obvious until my 30's. Personal expansion is a funny thing. We are given infinite opportunities to learn, grow, and evolve. The catch, though, is the opportunities become more challenging the longer it takes to learn the lesson. They may show up as the tickle of a feather or a gentle nudge. Unlearned lessons may return as a whack on the back of the head and then a punch to the arm. Then comes the punch to the gut, then the face, then the private parts. Sometimes the universe winds up and throws the good old twat punch just to ensure you got it this time.

My experiences in my early twenties consisted of college life, travel abroad, occasional boyfriends, and partying with friends. Because we were *all* figuring things out and witnessing our childhood beliefs and patterns play out into adulthood, mine weren't as glaring until later in life. By my mid to late twenties (having already had two or three dysfunctional relationships under my belt), my friends began to follow a similar trajectory as one another—meet a successful guy, get married, settle down, have children. I continued my trajectory of perpetuating my unhealthy childhood beliefs and patterns into adulthood. I began what turned out to be a successful career in education, but I continued to *party* and was having difficulty meeting that *right* guy. That's when my unhealthy beliefs and patterns began to manifest in more obvious ways.

By the time I was in my early 30's, I was not only *still* estranged from my father and that entire side of his family (and had been since I was a teenager), but I was now estranged from my mother, stepfather, and brother, who were really the only family I had left.

When I was 30 years old, I eloped with a guy with whom I had a bit of a tumultuous relationship. He was perfect! He fit snuggly with my "need" to be neglected. His neglect ignited my feelings of abandonment, woke up the fear, triggered my anger and inability to express it in a healthy way, thus exacerbating my feelings of unworthiness. Total fairy tale. Whenever he felt wronged by me and punished me with neglect, it was go time! I got to dig into my treasure chest of irrational beliefs about myself and relive my toxic patterns.

7

My personal favorite was *I believe that I am unworthy of love, so I always have to work harder to be loved.* I wrang the Shammy dry with that baby! Out of desperation to be loved, I'd pursue, he'd retract, and I would act out in anger, providing proof for all of my other irrational beliefs–and the cycle continued.

It fit like a glove, so I married him and was alienated from the only family I had left for about two years. Their premise for their side of the estrangement was that because I was so selfish, I didn't include them in the wedding. Truth be told, I eloped because I didn't think they cared and truly thought I was letting them off the hook. Regardless of how valid our individual truths were, we all were attached to our own belief systems and nothing was changing that.

I was divorced 11 months later, had no family, few friends, and was living alone 1,200 miles away from the place I was born and raised.

My 30's were rough. Still outwardly successful but internally, I was lonely, angry, and developing a pretty serious drug dependency. For years, I dated jerk after jerk after jerk, and what in my 20's would feel like a whack to the back of the head or a punch to the arm, turned into twat punch after twat punch after twat punch.

The opportunities to recognize my beliefs and patterns and reconcile my imbalances were infinite, but because I had no idea that it was ME creating these experiences through MY beliefs about MYSELF and what I deserved in life, I just continued the patterns, attracting to me what I believed aligned with my worthiness.

By my mid 30's, I reconciled my strained and distant relationship with my mother. I went back to tolerating my stepfather, and I never really mended fences with my brother. Because of his own dysfunction, he was never able to connect with me, blamed me for our family's woes and was blatant about it, always looking for a reason to communicate his disgust for me. Needless to say, visiting New Jersey was never a comfortable assignment.

It was just so frustrating because it felt like I was following all of the "rules": I was educated, respected in my career, self-sufficient, owned my own home, was debt free, had cool hobbies, was athletic, attractive, and generous with my friends, but I was so lonely and empty, without purpose, and internally in deep despair.

I honestly could not figure out why I couldn't have the love and the lives that my friends had. I always knew on some level that I was different from them. I even understood that my life's circumstances played a huge role in my differing perspectives and personal development, but I never really understood what to do to create a different life for myself. Frankly, I didn't understand or even believe that I could.

Here is a very important piece of information that I've learned along the way that helps me make sense of the events and consequences of events in our lives: *Nothing is isolated.* Everything builds on everything else. It is all cause-and-effect relationships, and it just takes a catalyst to reveal the intensity of that moment.

Nobody just pees their pants. You hold it, ignore it, pass on a bathroom opportunity, do the dance and ignore it some more. Then, one sneeze, and you have to change your drawers. It was never the sneeze. The sneeze was just the catalyst that revealed the intensity of the momentum of ignoring what your body needed.

This momentum of unchecked beliefs and patterns that we carry with us can become so intense and so powerful that the slightest catalyst can unveil a treasure trove of experiences of trauma and drama that can appear random, tragic, and often unfair. The reality, however, is we attract these experiences over and over until we learn the lesson, and the longer it takes to learn the lesson, the more momentum that comes with that lesson.

To reverse this momentum, it is like stopping a rolling car on an incline. The longer the car rolls, the more momentum it gains. First, you must stop the car. It will continue to push you back, but with attention, force, and commitment, you can slow it to a stop. Then, you must push it forward and up the incline. At first, it'll take big strides and strong footing. You may even get toppled backward once or twice, but with commitment and endurance, your footing will become stronger, and the pace will become quicker, creating a steady momentum in the opposite direction. Eventually, the terrain will flatten out and the pushing will become less intense, and at some moments, the car will feel as if it's rolling on its own, fueled by its own momentum and the occasional nudge from the rear.

This shift in momentum can be an arduous task, but once that car is moving, you can hop in, pop the clutch, and steer that mother fucker wherever you want it to go! At this point, all it needs is some fuel and some general maintenance.

I began the shift in my momentum in 2008 when I was 37 years old. Because of my loneliness, in 2006, I bought a Shih-tzu because, regardless of the rules of my condo association, I, well, I was getting a dog!

By 2007, I was found out and began getting the dreadful condo association letters, and by 2008, I sold my condo and bought a house in the same neighborhood. The shift was a big one. It was necessary and done out of the love for Princess Mia, but at the time, I didn't realize the dominos that I began to topple.

When I moved to my new home, I shifted my focus from my loneliness and inability to find a man to "complete me" to creating a beautiful new home for myself and Miss Mia. I exchanged my bar hopping and dating that always ended in disappointment for interior decorating and landscaping that ignited my creativity. I also exchanged my self-medicating with drugs and food and excessive exercising (that I believed would reverse the damage of my former lifestyle) for healthier habits that contributed to a more mindful and heart centered lifestyle. For months, I shopped, painted, landscaped, and redecorated. I worked on that house, creating a foundation for my new life there, unbeknownst to me that I was shifting the energy that I had been sitting in for most of my thirties. In those months, I was able to stop the car and reverse it, but the real work was still ahead of me.

Part II: Reversing the Momentum

My relationship with my mother had always been tenuous at best. There was definitely emotional distance between us, and as I came into womanhood, there were undertones of competition that I never fully identified or understood but felt on a deeper level. I had lived on my own since I was 18 years old, returning home for Christmas and summers and hosted the occasional visit from her, but there was no real warmth or closeness that I can remember.

After we reconciled our estrangement when I was in my early to mid-30's, we established a relationship that was built on the foundation of two new lines drawn in the sand. The relationship felt like it included a new level of respect, maybe even friendship, but no real warmth or even love.

Remember, my mother had so many toxic beliefs about herself and the world around her that continued to be met with whacks and punches (in the you know what) for her learning, but the lessons went unlearned and the changes weren't made and the momentum continued in the same direction, only exacerbating her acrimonious disposition and tainted worldview.

At this point in our lives, we were very much in

alignment and spoke often. We commiserated about all of the things we hated about our lives, mostly our jobs, and gossiped about all the people that had wronged us in one way or another. In essence, we were encapsulated in a codependent, anti-personal growth bubble that was comfortable for both of us at the time. I was so pleased to finally have a relationship with my mother that I never really took time to notice that its foundation was based on fear, anger, and discontent.

When I was thirty-seven and bought my house and reestablished my priorities, my energy began to change, and I began to shift the momentum of my own toxicity. Shortly after, I met my daughters' birth father and had two children within sixteen months of one another and truly experienced unconditional love for the first time in my life.

The birth of my children, creating this new experience of unconditional love, afforded me a whole new set of experiences and opportunities to examine my beliefs about my mother.

When I was first pregnant, my mother was all in. She was excited and wanted to help me in any way she could (from 1,200 miles away, of course). Her eagerness to help stemmed mostly from my "needing" her. From my mother's perspective, I appeared to be in an undesirable situation, and in some respects, I was, and she could resonate with that.

The details of my relationship with Luis were a bit sordid, and my mother embraced the ability to judge me for it—Luis and I weren't married, he was much younger than me, he was of a different ethnicity and culture, and 'had nothing to offer' financially. Also, both of my pregnancies were complicated. I experienced a loss of a twin during the first pregnancy, which was on the heels of a miscarriage, and I was carrying a baby with a congenital heart defect during the second pregnancy. Not to mention, six months into that pregnancy and a few weeks after I discovered my daughter's CHD, I discovered Luis had been cheating on me with a variety of women throughout our entire relationship while I was financially supporting him and his educational pursuits. It appeared to be quite the disaster, and my mother thrived in these situations. She felt most comfortable in the discomfort; she could relate, and in some ways feel better about herself because in her eyes my life sucked, too.

After the birth of my children, none of these concerns mattered to me. I understood that my circumstances weren't ideal, but by this point, this was the standard I had set for myself. To some degree, I came to accept that this was just the way my life looked. Also, my children were amazing and healthy(ish) and elicited a feeling of unconditional love in me that was beyond measure. I was so smitten with being their Mommy that nothing else mattered.

I had noticed, however, a dissonance beginning to reestablish itself between my mother and me. The reason why was unclear at the time, but in retrospect, now that I experienced motherhood firsthand, I began for the first time (while pushing forty) to internally question my mother's motives and maternal actions.

Knowing how I felt about my children and what motherhood meant to me, I couldn't reconcile my mother's inconsistencies. I couldn't understand how a mother who loved her children could behave in many of the ways she had behaved over the years. What was once an undertone that I neither questioned nor grasped entirely was now glaringly obvious to me, and once I opened my eyes and saw it, I could not unsee it. For the first time, I began to question my childhood experiences. I began to question my beliefs about her, about me, and about the world around me. My eyes were now open—the evidence was everywhere.

For my babies' first couple of years, my focus was primarily on pregnancies, birthing children, ending the relationship with the girls' father (for obvious reasons), and handling my younger daughter's medical complications, while holding both a full and part-time job to support the circus I was calling my life.

For a long time, I remained amicable with the girls' father, continued to support him in any way I could, and continued to embrace him as a part of our family for the sake of my daughters. I carried a lot of pain, anger, and resentment but had enough clarity to understand the importance of nurturing that relationship, especially since I had been without my own father for about twenty-five years at that point.

After the birth of my children, my mother visited more regularly—approximately every two to three months—and appeared to be a supportive force, but on some level reveled in the drama of my life, not in a malicious way but in a familiar homey way, like she was most comfortable there. She had embraced a relationship with Luis and offered him support in any way she could. She said it brought her comfort in knowing she could help the girls by helping Luis be a better father.

In hindsight, I understand that what we do for others is never really about them as much as it is about us. Our doing for others reflects how we see ourselves when we offer that assistance. What is our true motivation?

I believe my mother's motivation was partly what she claimed mixed with a dab of feeling better about herself for "doing charity" along with a touch of satisfaction in undermining me. I've witnessed her do this before with my "rivalries", but for this one, I was front and center and now saw it with clear vision.

In February 2012, my younger daughter had her first open heart surgery that had been promised to her since she was airlifted to Miami Children's Hospital upon delivery the year before. While planning and anticipating this surgery in the weeks prior, I received what turned out to be a hand delivered letter at my place of employment, wait for it....from my father! Just to set the tone—estrangement at fourteen years old, a brief failed reconciliation at eighteen years old, I am now forty years old. By this point, the twat punches were coming hard and fast.

His note read,

"Dear Dana, I am in town for two weeks, and I would love

to see you." There was some logistical information after that, and then he closed with, *"Not a single day goes by that I don't think about you. Love, Dad."*

Then something strange happened. I now attribute it to my newly opened and loving heart. Once I got past the initial feelings of panic, fear, and angst and reminded myself that I was not a fourteen-year-old girl, rather, I was a grown woman with two children of my own, I took a deep breath and called him.

My response to those of my friends who knew my story and *The Legend of Joe Sardano*, who dumbfoundedly asked why I would agree to see him, was that this man exhibited such courage after all these years, that who was I to reject his desire to see me while he entered the golden years of his life? What I didn't realize was how this one moment of unconditional love and forgiveness would increase the momentum of my life in the direction that I had always desired.

So, in the week prior to my thirteen-month-old daughter having full open-heart surgery, I had my father over for lunch. I introduced him to my home, my life, the forty-year-old version of Dana Sardano, and his two beautiful granddaughters.

We had a lovely time. We only spoke of the present.

He was completely enchanted by my children, and then we said goodbye. My father lived out of the country most of the year and returned two to three months every spring to see his accountant, his doctors, and then return home. It was the perfect, nonthreatening, "squirrel feeding" type of relationship for me. The relationship evolved at a comfortable rate, and the communication and visits increased in number, but initially, the concept of seeing him once a year totally sweetened the deal.

So now my father was gone, my mother had flown down to Florida for Nadia's surgery, and the circus was officially back in town. On the surface, my mother appeared understanding of the reconciliation with my father, but festering beneath the façade was all of her anger, resentment, and just plain rancor for the man. She occasionally stirred up and sprinkled in horror stories of him from my childhood but was clearly working over-time to contain herself. However, her passive aggressive tendencies were now kicking into high gear. What began as subtle and not so subtle jabs about my father, quickly graduated into overcompensation with unnecessary and completely irrational gifts for me and the girls. It was becoming quite uncomfortable to be around her.

Understanding her motivation, I attempted to diffuse

the situation by not speaking of him. I even went as far as identifying him with an alias in my phone. Because his involvement was never an issue when I was younger, I hadn't realized how threatened she was by his existence in my life. Although this experience did remind me that our reconciliation when I was eighteen failed primarily because of the guilt and pressure I received by her and my brother at that time.

That following fall, in comes Roberto Sgambellone, my future husband. Rob was different than the others. He was all of the things a woman could want in a man. I was a little confused by him at first because guys like Rob did not fit any of my patterns, but I did understand on some level that my forgiveness of my father somehow created a clear and open path for him to enter my life.

Rob was amazing! He was seriously everything I had ever wanted and needed from a partner, and he just adored the girls as they did him. He also understood that I was resolute in keeping a tightly knit relationship with Luis, and I planned to include him and his new significant other in all of our celebrations. Rob understood that Luis and I had committed to raising these children together, like a great big, blended family of sorts and was totally onboard.

As much as I attempted to pump the brakes on this new

relationship for the sake of protecting my children, the relationship moved rather quickly. Within six months, we were building an addition on my house. By nine months, we were engaged, and a year later we were married. It was quickly becoming the happiest time of my life.

Something very interesting happens when you make decisions that serve your highest good, decisions that create expansion and lift you to a happier, more fulfilling state of being. You begin to feel the dissonance with those people with whom you were previously in alignment. It gets quite uncomfortable, mostly because of our attachments to these relationships.

Your loved ones may not even realize, but through words and actions, they attempt to keep you with them in their state of being. They are just as attached to the relationship dynamic as you are (were), likely even more so. If we are not paying attention while in these situations, it could become easy to take the bait, but when we recognize what it is, we can choose the trajectory that best serves us and respond appropriately to the bait, if we choose to respond at all.

When I met and married Rob, my relationship attachments that couldn't stand to see me detach, released the most epic chum bucket of triggers that one could imagine.

The water was just ripe with blood flotsam, and with every chunk, I was forced to make some of the most difficult decisions of my life, one chunk at a time.

Part III: The Real Work

To offer some clarity with chronology, Rob and I began dating in October 2012 and were married by June 2014. The first few months of our relationship took us right through the holiday season, which made it super easy for everyone to remain peacefully involved with one another's lives and allowed me to steer my blended family vision, by orchestrating our "togetherness" down to the last detail.

At this point, Luis had a new significant other, and we all spent Thanksgiving together. Gifts were exchanged for Christmas, and Luis' plus-one even joined our birthday celebration for our two-year-old child in January. I was so full of myself, thinking that I had actually created something beautiful out of what appeared to be a stinky pile of shit.

Without realizing my pattern, however, I had spent my entire life people pleasing with my mother (and all subsequent relationships), and although I thought I was running the show, I was exhibiting the same behavior with

Luis under the guise of *the girls must have a relationship with their father*. Yes, I was including him so that he could be a part of the girls' lives, but I was also steeped in fear and trying to control everything by doing all the legwork to create our blended family, handling all of their medical and personal business, receiving ZERO financial support for the girls, and feeling frustrated and put upon for doing so. I was unwittingly perpetuating my *working for love* pattern to get the girls the love that I believed they needed, which was based on my pattern of the love that *I* so desperately needed. Psychology is so complicated!

Rather quickly, I began to sense that Luis' lady friend did not appreciate my gestures of friendship and Luis' resistance to any cooperative parenting became more evident. Shortly after Nadia's birthday in January 2013, the dissonance became blatantly obvious and the gloves came off.

I pushed. He resisted. There was a falling out, and in March 2013, Luis fell off the map. He refused to come around because I was "baby mama drama", and my biggest fear of my children becoming abandoned by their father was coming true.

During the months prior to this falling out, my mother had a few opportunities to break bread with all of us as a *blended* family, and I immediately witnessed a shift in her demeanor. She began to take undermining me in front of my friends to a whole new level. Her discomfort with my new-found happiness became palpable, and it manifested in belittling behavior and the undermining of not only my home but also my position within the house. When she had an audience, she would make jokes about me, often in front of me, and she would fawn all over Luis' girlfriend to the point of discomfort of the bystanders.

One time she disappeared to the casino, a behavior that was not uncommon for her, but when she returned with winnings, she pulled Luis aside and handed him money, also a common occurrence, and joked, "Don't tell Dana I gave you money. Take your girlfriend out to a nice dinner," only to later joke about this side conversation in mixed company in front of me!

Yeah, my mother's behavior became real irrational rather abruptly. At the time, I found it hurtful and confusing, but I understand now that my mother's extreme dysfunction was exacerbated by my determination to break free from my paradigms. I was freeing myself from the familiar toxic roles that we all played, but I never sent out a memo to warn anybody. As a result, my mother was acting out. So, now that Luis was clearly dissenting from the family, it was time to choose sides, and that she did.

After Luis spent an entire month completely off the grid, he contacted me because he wanted to see the girls, who were now two and three years old. At this point, I had to make some very difficult decisions, not based on my old beliefs and patterns, but rather on the new trajectory that I had chosen for myself. Now it's the battle of beliefs that stir in my head: *What do I believe is best for the girls?* vs. *What will people say about my mothering?*

THIS is the "work" people talk about in personal and spiritual growth–NOT the dancing in fields under the moonlight with a crystal in each hand but the gut wrenching, unpopular decisions that contradict the masses and all you've ever known.

After much consideration, I asked myself the following questions:

- **What is the evidence here?**

The evidence is the moment the circumstances became uncomfortable, Luis took off and returned at his convenience regardless of the effect it could have on the children.

- **What does it tell me?**

This behavior and other similar behaviors tell me that this is his pattern and that this will likely happen again and again.

- **What do I want?**

What I want is for my children to be well, happy, and whole, without abandonment issues.

- **How do I get there?**

To get there, I first told Luis that he will now not be permitted to see the children without first getting a lawyer. I then filed for child support, and I remained steadfast in my decision, regardless of what the critics had to say.

The line was drawn in the sand. My position was clear. The rest was up to Luis.

Six months passed, he tried showing up without warning after a party for Nahla's birthday. No lawyer. I sent him away.

Four months later, he contacted me on Christmas. No lawyer. I sent him away.

Three months later, a year after he disappeared the first time, because of a glitch in the system, he received his first child support notice. Immediately after that, he contacted a lawyer. I was now open to discussion through our attorneys and awaiting his next move.

Here's what happens when we decide to shift the momentum of our patterns. The players with whom we have been involved will continue to play by the old rules, expecting us to do the same. It's not anybody's fault. This is just how it is. Often feelings of guilt and obligation seep in, but the reality is, we don't owe anybody anything. No explanation. No grand declarations. Just commitment to ourselves and what's in *our* highest good.

In this circumstance, my children not having a fear of abandonment and a lack of trust and the myriad of other beliefs about themselves and the world as a result of his inconsistent visitation was my first priority. The opinions of others were endless—the "How could you…" and the "But it's their father…" were not in short supply, especially from my mother, but at the end of the day, I had to make the difficult decision based on what I felt was just and in the best interest of my children, regardless of what the previous (unhealthy) version of myself would do. This was one of the most difficult decisions I had made up to that point; however, the personal strength and empowerment that resulted from my resolve set me up for what was coming next.

In that year of Luis' absence, life just continued to

become more and more beautiful. Rob and I built a breathtaking addition to our family's home, and we got engaged that summer. We were cultivating a beautiful little family of our own. The children were thriving. This was truly the happiest time of my life.

My mother, however, was still immersed in the old way of being and playing by the rules of the previous versions of ourselves, and the happier I became, the greater the dissonance between us. I didn't see her very often, but it was becoming quite uncomfortable to be around her, as her acting out steadily increased.

Finally, in the spring of 2014, a few months before the wedding, I took a stand in a conversation and told her she owed me an apology, a new boundary for me. I truly had never spoken up to her in that way prior to this instance, which to be honest, seemed insignificant to me at the time. This new line in the sand turned out to be the first salvo in a battle royale that would result in my never speaking to my mother again.

The details are complex and unnecessary, but the moment my mother had been given permission to be outwardly angry with me, all hell broke loose; it was as if she had been waiting for her cue. My stepfather and brother, who had always followed my mother's lead, had also been waiting to be let off the chain, and once they were, it got ugly, like I still shake my head in disbelief as I type these words, ugly. Not only did my mother not come to my bridal shower and not inform anyone, but for a month, not one of them responded to my wedding invitation. My stepfather left me a voicemail informing me that he would not be walking me down the aisle because of my abuse of my mother, and my brother sent me several emails (all sanctioned by my mother), which most likely had been formulating in his head for years prior, about how disgusting I was. It was a bit paradoxical—shocking but not at all surprising at the same time.

In the same paradoxical fashion—I was truly devastated but relieved at the same time. It was extremely painful and confusing because I still carried many of those irrational beliefs about myself from childhood. I was so completely torn up by the whole experience that my husband spent every day literally picking me up off the floor, trying to help me understand that the behavior that I had become so accustomed to was indeed unhealthy and irrational and that I had done nothing to deserve this. It took months for me to recover from this incident, but before I got married, I had to make ANOTHER decision that was contradictory to previous versions of myself but was for my highest good.

Prior to this fall out, out of respect to the fragility of my mother, stepfather, and brother, I sat my father down and told him that I would not be inviting him or his brother and his family, my uncle and cousins, to my wedding because I didn't want to upset my mother. My father returned home after that visit disappointed, but he understood.

I never felt right about that decision. I actually felt it sit like a weight in the pit of my stomach, but at the time, it felt like "the right thing to do." I still had one foot in each world and felt a loyalty to my mother, regardless of what I was currently experiencing. In hindsight, my belief based on that loyalty was not rational, but that's what irrational belief systems are—just that, irrational.

After weeks of fall-out from asking for an apology from my mother, I finally listened to my gut and called my father and invited him, knowing that if my mother came around and they both showed up, my wedding would be Chernobyl. I told him nothing, just apologized for making a bad call and asked him to come, and without hesitation he did, and the heaviness immediately disappeared.

THESE are the difficult decisions. These situations bring out the worst of critics and create sides and end friendships, but these are the decisions that strengthen that momentum toward peace and freedom. Listening to your heart and ignoring the voices that tell you otherwise is the work.

Rob and I were married in June 2014. My father was there. My mother was not. People had opinions. It was the greatest day of my life.

In the few years following my wedding, there was no real contact between me and my maternal side of the family. There were a handful of attempts to pull me into their hornet's nest, but I refused the invitations, and they dissolved as quickly as they appeared. It was truly ugly, but I had to decide what I believed about my own worthiness, and I had to behave in ways that were in alignment with that. It was rough, but I had to do the work. Period.

My mother passed away in August 2017, having not seen her grandchildren since March 2014. Throughout this experience with my mother, I consistently made decisions that aligned with my self-worth and highest good. I consistently dealt with the pain of heartbreak and loss. I did the work. I have no regrets. The momentum of my life is now full speed ahead.

Part IV: Reaping the Rewards

I always understood that a level of clarity emerges when we clear out the confusion and self-doubt that clouds our existence, but what I have experienced in the years subsequent to my wedding is truly astounding.

A year after Luis attained legal counsel, in August 2015, he signed over his legal rights to the girls, was absolved of all financial responsibility, and on that same day, Rob legally adopted them. My greatest desire for my children was that they'd live in a stable home where they felt safe and with loving parents they could trust. I was always committed to breaking the cycle of abuse and neglect, and although at times it appeared that I was not doing so, I was steadfast in what I desired and made decisions that were in alignment with that desire. This allowed me to live with a beautiful family and a beautiful home filled with love, trust, and laughter. Life was truly beautiful!

Rob and I had a wonderful babysitter that we loved and trusted, who would watch the girls on Friday evenings. What began as early dinners and then home to the girls quickly devolved into Costco or Target runs and then home for early bedtime.

One Friday evening in January 2015, I felt the urge to do something different. I saw an ad for one of those wine and paint classes and suggested to Rob that we go. He scoffed at the notion of hanging out with a bunch of ladies, drinking wine, and painting on a Friday night, but he welcomed the idea of going to *Michael's,* the local craft store, grabbing a bunch of supplies and painting at home. So that's what we did!

That evening, something was ignited within my core that I could never do justice with words. My creativity, that had lain dormant for thirty years, having been trumped by my survival instincts, had been awoken through my feelings of love, safety, and security. My new-found peace and freedom allowed me to stoke the flames of this rediscovered creativity. In essence, I completely lost my mind! I was compelled to paint and painted every single day. Painting brought me so much joy, and I now had the freedom to follow that joy. Every evening after work, I would come home, make dinner, put the children to bed, put a sheet over the dining room table and paint. I painted feverishly. For about six months, I would search for pictures and replicate them in my own style, and then one day, I painted the image of a mother and child and found my voice. Then, I became crazed. I had paintings everywhere: they covered the walls in my home, they covered the walls in my office at school—I was giving them away to anybody who showed interest. I went full Oprah Winfrey on it! I was all, "YOU get a painting! And YOU get a painting! EVERYBODY gets a painting!" Then, someone offered to pay me for one, which kicked my momentum into high gear.

By 2016, I was entering art festivals and had begun exhibiting my art in local restaurants, art galleries, and local studios. By 2017, I left my 23-year career in education to pursue a career as an artist. By 2019, I opened a gallery of my own, where I sit right now and write this book!

The story of my journey of creativity is far more deserving than just citing three events with three sentences; however, my beautiful story of self-discovery can be shared another day. What is important here is the catalyst to this extreme shift in trajectory and the propelled momentum of that trajectory.

The psychological term *fight or flight* response is very common in our culture, expressing the human response to danger. People, when they feel threatened, either fight or fly, and in some cases even freeze. We all identify with at least one of these reactions, but what we often don't consider is that we are born with this instinct to keep us safe when we are at our most vulnerable. These instincts have been hard wired into our cellular structure in order to keep us safe from danger. As we grow, learn, and develop into more complex thinking and feeling creatures, our need for survival should expand into a more complex way of being, which includes, a sense of identity, our passion for life, and the ability to openly love without condition or expectation. We should ultimately embrace our own authenticity, embrace our internal wisdom, and trust our intuition, which leads to our self-actualization, which ultimately leads us to peace and freedom.

What often happens, unfortunately, is we become stunted by our uncomfortable and sometimes even tragic personal experiences and are left utilizing our fight or flight responses throughout our course of development. This hinders our personal growth, keeping us from true peace and freedom.

What I've gained through my own unpleasant and yes sometimes tragic experiences, were opportunities to expand my consciousness through adjusting my reactions, opportunities to revisit my coping mechanisms and ultimately to alter my perspectives of these experiences. By doing so and reversing the trajectory of my suffering and disempowerment, by doing the work to propel and push this momentum, and through maintaining these practices, I have found myself, and continue to find myself in a place of peace and freedom.

My hope is that by reading this book, you will find your way to yours.

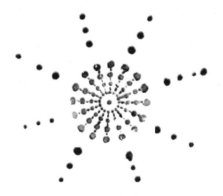

First Recommandment

I Shalt not claim victimhood.

Rather, I SHALL recognize that the power to create my experience is always within me. There are no victims, just opportunities to learn and grow, and I choose to learn from each opportunity.

As I observe my surroundings, I can't help but notice the extreme polarity in beliefs and perspectives. I also can't help but notice that the media and all avenues that bring us information only exacerbate this polarity.

As an artist whose strength lies in color theory, it is difficult to wrap my brain around the rigidity of this line of thinking. If the only two colors that get any airtime are black and white, then what is the purpose of all of the other colors?

I also wonder about all of the hybrid colors. Sometimes when I intend to use the color blue, I use more than one shade of blue to create that color. Not only that, I often add some green, and even have been known to throw in an unlikely color like red or pink that often goes unnoticed in the big picture but lends to the layering and dimension of the overall color.

What happens when the observer looks at the painting is they perceive the blue, notice the nuances from different angles, and enjoy the depth and interest of the color without always understanding why. However, upon further inspection, the observer may notice the green or even the red, but to the naked eye, it's blue. It's just blue.

If the observer likes blue, then great, but if the observer doesn't care for blue or even has an adverse emotional reaction to blue, it is not so great. If the observer doesn't care to take the time to analyze the color from different angles or perspectives, they may never have the opportunity to truly appreciate the work of art that is right in front of their very eyes.

I have learned through my experience as an artist and as a human being that nothing is ever JUST one thing. We, as human beings, have developed the habit of categorizing things because that's how our brain helps us understand and feel safe among our surroundings, but we are so much more than the comfortable category in which we place things.

Those of you that are reading this book understand that I am an author and an artist. Those are easy categories in which to place myself—familiar and nonthreatening, right? But anyone who truly knows me, anyone who has taken the time to experience me from different angles and different perspectives understands that there is so much more to me. I'm an educator, a mother, a sister, a wife, a daughter, a friend, an ex-girlfriend, a cancer survivor. I am also a truth teller, a lie teller, a coward, a warrior, an intellectual, an athlete, a smart ass, a joker, smoker, a midnight toker—the list goes on. I am an amalgamation of all of my experiences, thoughts, beliefs, behaviors, and paradigms, and it would be unfair to observe me for a single moment in time and say, "Yeah, that's blue."

Not only would that be unfair, but it would also be unfair to have experienced me for a brief time in 1991 or 2004 or 2019 and decide that now in this moment, "Yeah, that's blue." Nothing is EVER just one thing, EVER, and when we come to realize that about ourselves, our relationships, and the world around us, it becomes easier to release our judgements, and our experience becomes so much richer and more enjoyable.

In 2015, my husband adopted my children. Their birth father, who was unable to father them in the way these children needed at the time, *courageously* stepped aside and allowed Rob and me to raise them together as a family in the way that we saw as appropriate and for their highest good. This transition was tumultuous and emotionally driven on all levels. There were many components, many pitfalls along the way, and many unsolicited opinions as well.

My narrative is that I did everything I possibly could to make decisions that best served my children, and although I'm sure that there were missteps along the way, I attest to the integrity of this statement. There are many people in my inner circle who will also attest to this statement. Today, my children will attest to this statement. However, there are many people that will vehemently contradict this statement, and at some point, maybe even tomorrow, my children might become two of those people.

You see, my fairy-tale story of how my children were adopted by their father was not painted in black or white or even one shade of blue. There were a myriad of colors and varied artists that collaborated with this story, all sharing their own thoughts, beliefs, perspectives, and paradigms and each bringing their own paint sets to boot. My story will never be JUST one thing.

So why does this matter?

My takeaway is that observing a situation is different than experiencing a situation, which is different than reflecting on a situation. The more angles and perspectives we take to look at something, the more shades of blue we are able to perceive, thus enriching our experience.

Victim/Victor

When we choose to categorize our observations and experiences into a category—usually it's either this or that, black or white, us against them, victim or victor—we rob ourselves of truly understanding and experiencing the experience, and by doing this, we rob ourselves of the opportunity to learn and grow from it.

In my narrative of my children's adoption, I could easily have painted myself as the victim in the end rising to victory, but I would have lost all sight of what was truly important: the emotional health and wellness of my children.

Many of us, myself included, have spent much of our lives caught up in this paradigm.

"Can you believe what she/he did to me?"

"Why do people always mistreat me?"

"If he/she/they hadn't done this to me, I wouldn't be in this situation."

The list of complaints about what *they* did to *me* is

endless. I have been *victimized* by the people in my life for as long as I can remember.

How do I make it stop?

STEP 1 is to understand that this belief we carry about the world is pervasive in society. News organizations, advertising, television programming, politics, sporting events, the list goes on, all thrive under this paradigm. You must pick a side and remain loyal to that side. Anything else is nonsensical and even shameful.

But is it? Is it nonsensical to have the ability to see more than one facet of a situation?

Is it shameful to exercise discernment and see and even understand where people are coming from?

Is it crazy to try to understand that most people, without even realizing, are walking around with irrational belief systems and coping mechanisms from childhood that no longer serve them and are vehemently protecting these belief systems and coping mechanisms through their own words and actions?

Is it an outlandish concept to think if we all recognized this about ourselves and began taking the steps to "deprogram" and empower ourselves that we would not only be a part of the solution, but we'd also have a deeper understanding of ourselves and the world around us as well as the ability to show compassion for those around us that just don't quite yet understand this?

Is it shameful to want to change a system of beliefs and a society of broken paradigms that is no longer serving any of us?

The separation of the masses into factions that inherently attack one another or defend themselves is not a novel concept. The feeding of that fear to divide the masses into submission is not new to the history books either. The question is why are WE, the people, STILL falling for it?

I could offer a laundry list of theories, but I'd prefer to solve the problem through a practical approach to personal empowerment.

STEP 2 is to remember this Recommandment: **I Shalt not claim victimhood. Rather, I SHALL recognize that the power to create my experience is always within me. There are no victims, just opportunities to learn and grow, and I choose to learn from each opportunity.**

Our falling "victim" to the behaviors of others runs deep. Our experiences begin in childhood, where we develop our patterns, beliefs, and coping mechanisms, and they begin with those who reared us, who developed their patterns, beliefs, and coping mechanisms from those who reared them, who developed their patterns, beliefs, and coping mechanisms from those who reared them. Get the picture?

Your parents, siblings, family, neighbors, teachers, whoever "victimized" you, did not do anything TO YOU. They behaved in a way that was in alignment with their own (irrational) patterns, beliefs, and coping mechanisms. We are all operating from the place of that hurt, scared, and sometimes even broken child within. ALL of us!

STEP 3 is to accept these truths and release fear, pain, and judgement from your experiences that you hold in your heart. Forgive those who "victimized" you. Forgive those who "victimized" them, and forgive yourself for doing the same, for none of you knew better. Because if you knew better, you would have done better.

STEP 4 is to complete the steps offered in Recommandments Two and Three for releasing irrational beliefs and coping mechanisms that we've picked up in childhood.

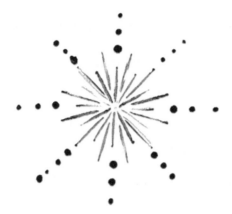

Second Recommandment

I shalt not become entrenched
in my emotions.

Rather, I SHALL trust my emotional guidance system and rely on this information to inform me of what I don't want in order to direct me to what I do want.

I often wonder, when did we stop listening to ourselves? When did we stop listening to our inner voice, our own sense of judgement about things? Our own guidance system?

As babies, we allow our needs to drive us, and we quickly learn how to manipulate our surroundings and the people who care for us to give us what we need for survival. We cry, and we get fed. We scream, and we get changed. We coo, and we get held. We may appear completely helpless, but from the moment of delivery, and in many cases conception, WE are running the show, and we are doing it simply based on our own personal guidance system. How do I feel? What do I need? How do I get it? And as a result, we successfully manipulate the microcosm of our mini universe to ensure all our needs are met.

As we develop and our needs become a little more complicated, the methods we use to get what we need change with our development. When a baby cries, the caretakers fall all over themselves to stop that baby from crying, most often by figuring out what that baby needs and by quickly fulfilling that desire. As the baby develops into a toddler, the outcries may become stale and lack efficacy, so new tools are added to the baby's repertoire, such as kicking, screaming, and head banging.

From what I have gathered, this is when the shift in behavior begins. As a toddler is exploring new ways to get their needs met, the behaviors often become more egregious to the parents, who may not realize that these behaviors are just a means to an end for the child. The parent, often not understanding the toddler's motivation, acts out of desperation to silence the cries and extinguish the behaviors, thus teaching the child their first lesson in compliance. If a baby cries at bedtime in order to be held, and is held, their behavior is reinforced. When that same child, as a toddler, is ignored for the same behavior, not only do they question their own guidance system, but they experiment with more advanced behaviors—screaming, crib rocking, banging, perhaps. How this behavior is received sets the emotional and behavioral trajectory for that child.

As the toddler further develops, the experiments with behavior to receive their most basic needs continues, but as the child develops, so does the parent. The parent will teach the child what is acceptable and unacceptable behavior through rewards and consequences, getting what the child wants vs. not getting what they want. The child quickly learns through their external influences how to get what they want. This is a simple concept that we often overlook in adulthood.

As we develop as human beings, our needs and the ways in which we have them met change with each stage of development. As we become more complex, our behaviors as well as the emotions that guide us become more complex, but the end game is to always have our needs met.

What often happens, however, is sometimes the emotions that "guide" us to have our needs met can be so intense and so overwhelming that we lose sight of our "need" and become entrenched in the emotion that was intended to lead us to it in the first place.

Simply put, if a child acts out in anger because they become fearful of a stranger, and the caretaker, having little understanding of the reason for the anger, addresses the emotion rather than the need, then two things happen:

1. The child carries a fear memory from that experience that could develop into an *irrational* belief about themselves or the experience, ie: When I become angry, I am unworthy of help or protection or my caretaker cannot be trusted to protect me or even when I express my needs, those who care for me will not meet them.

2. The child's needs are NOT met. The child learns that the emotional behavior is just that, an expression of emotion with no resolution. In every experience, pleasant or unpleasant, the child has an opportunity to learn how to utilize and process an emotion to get their needs met. When the experience is cut off at the emotional component, the purpose of the emotional guidance system is stifled.

YOUR EMOTIONAL GUIDANCE SYSTEM is your greatest navigation system for getting all of your needs met. When used with awareness and acuity, you will become amazed at the mountains you can move through navigating this system.

Your guidance system comes in two simple steps:

1. Feel and identify the emotion.

    a. How am I feeling? What am I feeling?

    b. The emotion, in varying degrees, is either going to feel good or bad.

2. Act on the emotion WITHOUT JUDGEMENT to get your needs met.

    a. If the emotion feels good, then it is alerting you to do more things like that.

    b. If the emotion feels bad, it is alerting you to do fewer things like that.

    c. Do not judge the experience, the players, or the emotion. The experience and the emotion attached to it are simply an opportunity to see what you don't like, to decide what you do like, and to then figure out how to get that need met. It's that simple.

EXAMPLE:

I invited my neighbors over for dinner. They came empty handed, were discourteous in conversation, and they left without saying thank you.

How did this make me feel?

I felt confused at first, then a little angry, then I felt as if they had taken advantage of my hospitality.

What do these emotions tell me?

They tell me that my neighbors and I do not share the same values, that it doesn't feel good for me to spend time with people that aren't in alignment with my personal practices, and that it would better serve me to spend more time with people with whom I am in alignment.

It is truly this simple! Unfortunately, when we are developing into adulthood, through unpleasant and traumatic experiences, we pick up **irrational beliefs, patterns, and paradigms** along the way that muck up our natural guidance system, and if these irrational beliefs, patterns, and paradigms go unchecked, they not only become a part of our experience, but they also become instrumental in creating future unpleasant experiences perpetuating a vicious cycle of emotional entrenchment.

IRRATIONAL BELIEF SYSTEMS are developed when our emotional guidance is somehow halted or interrupted. Let's make an assumption that our most natural state of being is contentment. When we feel discontent, our primary objective is to figure out now, in this moment, what is the best course of action to move in the direction of contentment.

With every experience, we have an opportunity to move toward contentment and to learn new ways of being content. The emotions that we feel in these experiences help us along in this process. It's kind of like the "hot/cold" game. When we experience unpleasant emotions, we are making decisions and having experiences that are moving away from contentment. When we are feeling pleasant emotions, we are moving toward contentment.

When we are developing as children and young adults, we often have experiences that feel out of our control, that make us feel unsafe or unworthy or unloved based on our age-appropriate perception of the experience, and in an effort to manufacture safety or worthiness or love, we develop age-appropriate, self-protecting coping mechanisms to meet these needs.

Just as an example, if a six-year-old child felt abandoned because their mother was often late picking them up from school, they might develop "clingy" habits to help them feel safe and loved. This child has not yet developed the reasoning ability or even the communication skills to think, reflect, discuss, and understand why this perpetual lateness is happening. The six-year-old brain only knows that "Mommy did not come to get me as promised. I cannot trust the adults who love and care for me. I feel unsafe. I must figure out how to make myself feel safe."

So, here's what happens next. This can be super obvious or super subtle, but as a result of this experience, this child has found a way to make themselves feel safe in this situation, but the emotion and belief attached to the experience stays with the child.

As the child develops, they will continue to apply their coping mechanism to situations that make them feel unsafe. By choosing "clingy" when they feel unsafe or abandoned, they may cling to their loved one in the experience. During their formative years with their family, this may be cause for concern, but likely accepted because there is love in the equation; however, as the child grows into a young adult, relationships become more complicated and this coping mechanism not only becomes ineffective, but it also creates more experiences of abandonment because clinginess tends to repel people and create more experiences of abandonment, which only exacerbates the feelings of abandonment and puts the coping mechanism of clinginess into high gear to only perpetuate the cycle and concretize the belief system that "I am not worthy of love, and if I love someone, they will eventually 'not show up' for me."

Left unchecked, this belief system will be carried throughout life and create a pattern of abandonment that will be repeated over and over again in varying degrees and in all aspects of their life—from their work relationships to their social relationships to their romantic relationships.

The previous example of the neighbors' discourteousness is a relatively benign example, but it is important to understand that these patterns, whether subtle or more obvious, creep into our lives on a regular basis, and when we understand the source from where we react or respond to these situations and alter that pattern, we then alter our personal growth trajectory.

In the discourteous neighbors situation, one option is to recognize that this is no longer a relationship in which I choose to participate because this relationship lacks symbiosis and then just kindly move on with grace.

Another option is to continue the relationship and continue the same behavior of overextending myself, which only creates a breeding ground for feelings of resentment and anger that will become exacerbated by this continued relationship. I would then wonder why people constantly disappoint me and why people aren't there for me, which again is just validating my feelings of victimization and my lack of worthiness.

With awareness of the situation and willingness to adjust my patterns, I personally change the trajectory of my life's path one experience at a time.

Looking for Solutions

Regardless of the intensity of the situation, at this point, many of our experiences have disappointed us to a point of frustration and despair:

- "No matter how hard I try, the outcome is always the same!"
- "Why do these things always happen to me?"
- "Why can't I find happiness?"

Your situation feels hopeless because this pattern is all you've ever really known. It feels like your life experiences are all independent of one another and that they are all happening to you, and in many cases, it feels like the source of your woes is external or that someone else is causing your misfortune. The reality is that every problem has a solution. If we could remember to use our emotional guidance system rather than become immersed in fear, anxiety and despair, we could maintain clarity so that the solutions flow more quickly and easily to us.

At this point, our patterns and belief systems have become such an integral part of who we are that we not only forget to question their validity, but we also protect them with denial, anger, and vehemence when these aspects of our identity become threatened. We become a bit paradoxical. On the one hand, we protect ourselves, our beliefs, and our patterns ferociously, but on the other hand, we live in such self-doubt and mistrust of our own system of guidance, we begin to look outward when truly, the answers are within us all along.

Take your power back:

1. TAKE A MOMENT and identify a relationship or situation in your life that does NOT bring you contentment. ASK YOURSELF how does it make you feel?

2. SEE IF YOU CAN IDENTIFY YOUR PATTERN OF BEHAVIOR and then see if you can trace it back to the experience that was the source of that pattern.

3. ASK YOURSELF with your fully developed and functional adult brain, what belief system did I

develop from this experience?

4. ASK YOURSELF, is this belief rational? Likely it is not rational. Likely, it was a means of coping at that stage in development. Likely, this belief system no longer serves you.

5. TAKE A MOMENT and restructure a more rational belief system that serves you as a healthy and functioning adult who is worthy, safe, and loved.

6. APPLY THIS NEW RATIONAL BELIEF SYSTEM to your life every time the old pattern shows up.

Reversing belief systems that no longer serve us takes awareness and consistency, and in the beginning stages will feel like a tremendous amount of work, but once the habit is developed, the practice becomes easier. The good news is most experiences come from the same root cause(s), so once they are identified and handled at the source, the patterns and consequences have a way of clearing up on their own. Yay!

Third Recommandment

I shalt not apply irrational belief
systems and toxic behavioral
patterns that no longer serve me
to my life experiences.

Rather, I SHALL recognize that these beliefs were acquired during a time of crisis, and the patterns were developed as a result to help make me feel safe. I understand that not only did I develop these patterns as self-protection, but also that this is what people do—we ALL protect ourselves, we ALL are protecting something, we ALL are doing this to feel safe, and when we recognize this and these patterns, we are one step closer to healing them. I also understand that I am now safe and don't need coping mechanisms that no longer serve me. I recognize that everything I do is based on beliefs, patterns, and paradigms that I developed during my formative years, and if I find pattern(s) in my behavior that aren't serving me, I trace them to the source of that pattern, and I can then put them to rest for good.

As we develop through adolescence and enter adulthood, our behavioral patterns that are birthed from our belief systems that are then developed in our formative years become the basis of our life experiences. These patterns then become a way of life for us, often without us even realizing that we've created these patterns ourselves. The following is an example of the variety of potential patterns birthed from one simple childhood belief:

Childhood belief: *My needs do not matter.*

1. **Continued pattern of** always putting other people's needs first.

2. **Continued pattern of** always getting the "short end of the stick".

3. **Continued pattern of** attracting "takers", always feeling like my kindness is taken for granted.

4. **Continued pattern of** overcompensating for people when they are not meeting my needs.

5. **Continued pattern of** disappointment and despair in inequitable relationships.

6. **Continued pattern of** not properly setting boundaries for myself.

7. **Continued pattern of** accepting less than I want or need in any given situation.

8. **Continued pattern of** not feeling comfortable or worthy of communicating my needs.

9. **Continued pattern of** settling for less than I desire.

10. **Continued pattern of** continuing relationships that no longer serve me because even though I feel taken for granted and this makes me uncomfortable, it is a feeling I recognize, so I stay.

Because we often understand on a superficial level why we are the way we are or why we behave the way we do but never examine our understandings with the intention of reversing them, we often acquiesce to this way of being with the notion of *because my mother…I am like this* or *because when I was a kid…happened, I am like this.* We often accept our fate and perpetuate the patterns, and by perpetuating the patterns, they become increasingly uncomfortable and ultimately evolve into feelings of hopelessness, depression, and despair.

Sometimes, a specific experience will act as a catalyst for change, and this one particular adversity somehow knocks us into action so that we eventually decide enough is enough. We commit to changing our present circumstance that is causing us so much grief in what is often a reactionary, emotionally-driven display. The problem, however, is sustainability, because when we address internal bleeding with a knee jerk band aid, the solution is momentary, and the problem doesn't get solved. In order to reverse the pattern, you MUST detect it, find the root cause, and stop the bleeding from the source.

We also carry so much shame for our patterns, but paradoxically, we passionately defend them. The moment we are challenged by a loved one about our behaviors, we defend these behaviors. We defend our involvements. We defend our position. We defend all of it, but in actuality, we are defending our shame. We are defending our hopelessness. We are defending our self-doubt and mistrust of ourselves because for some reason that is often beyond our comprehension, we continue these patterns that are not serving us, and this mistrust of ourselves ultimately leads us to look outward.

Rituals and Practices

Rituals and practices are appealing to so many of us. There is something about structure and organization that brings us feelings of comfort and safety. Having a plan is important because it helps us with focus and offers us the comfort of knowing (for the most part) what to expect.

Throughout the unexpected turns and fluidity of our daily experiences, when life throws those curve balls, you can stick to the plan and fall back on—gym at 8am, work at 9am, dinner at 6pm, and softball every Tuesday and Thursday.

There is also something comforting about knowing what day of the week it is and knowing what Tuesday "feels" like and what Tuesdays entail. Structure is crucial in children's lives to ensure their feelings of safety and security, and the importance of this foundation of structure is carried into adulthood and is essential for us to thrive. What often happens when we begin to doubt our inner wisdom and internal guidance is we become imbalanced and too reliant on external structure. The term OCD is thrown around a lot, but obsessive behavior can come from feeling powerless, resulting in hyper focusing on things to control.

When our developed behavioral patterns no longer serve us and become toxic, we often begin the search for safety and comfort, and the search is often outward. There is no shortage of helpful tips, tools, groups, and resources to help a misaligned person find a way back to center. There is a plenitude of books, videos, gurus, spiritual practices, religious institutions, psychologists, sociologists, therapists, nutritionists, life coaches, spiritual advisors, support groups, hotlines, clubs, organizations, social media memes—the list goes on and on—that assist in a person's return to center.

What happens, however, is that because we have become so mistrustful of our own internal guidance, we often put all of our eggs in these baskets, because clearly these baskets can be trusted more than the internal guidance with which we were born and used as infants to keep us alive, once again disempowering ourselves only to perpetuate our feelings of hopelessness and despair.

When did we stop listening to ourselves? Why are we following someone else's rules for happiness? Why aren't we making our own rules? Why aren't we empowering ourselves?

When we lean too hard on the rituals and practices (often created by others) that we've adopted with the hope that this will in some way "fix" our woes, we neglect our own decision-making skills. As a result, we will never have practices of our own—that are OURS—once again dis-empowering ourselves only to perpetuate our feelings of hopelessness and despair that often lead us to these rituals and practices in the first place.

As I've previously mentioned, we are all protecting

something, but when we begin to understand that when we locate the core of our feelings of insecurity and the beliefs and patterns birthed from this fearful place, we will no longer feel compelled to protect ourselves and our outdated ineffective behavioral patterns. Rather, we can realign ourselves with beliefs and patterns that reflect our feelings of safety, worthiness, confidence, love, authenticity, intuition, and overall connectedness. When we are able to do this, we can engage in rituals and practices that bring us comfort and joy and that are OURS, empowering ourselves to live lives filled with love, peace, and freedom.

Fourth Recommandment

I shalt not ignore my chakra health.

Rather, I SHALL recognize that when I tend to the seven energy centers of my inner world, my outer world reflects that internal health and wellness.

What are the chakras, you ask?

Chakra is a Sanskrit term that means "wheel" or "disk" and is derived from the root word "cakra". Chakras are the concentrated energy centers of the body that are displayed as spinning wheels of energy or light. They are responsible for taking in, incorporating, and emanating energy to keep us functioning at optimal levels.

There are seven major chakras in the human body. Each chakra or energy center represents a different function and is represented by a different color. For example, your root chakra, which is represented in red, encompasses feelings of safety and security; your sacral chakra, orange, encompasses your creativity; your solar plexus, yellow, represents your empowerment, etc.

Chakras have become more common to the general public with the growth in popularity of yoga and New

Age philosophies in more recent years. However, first mentioned in the Vedas, ancient sacred texts of spiritual knowledge dating from 1500 to 1000 BC, this complex and ancient energy system originated in India thousands of years ago.

There is much one can study about the chakras, but for the sake of efficacy, I intend to focus on the practicality of chakras and how experiences, behaviors, and environmental factors can affect their health and how their health can affect your life.

The first three chakras are the root, sacral, and solar plexus. Their growth and expansion usually develop concurrently with the child's development and are responsible for feelings of safety and security, empowered creativity, confidence and a sense of identity. Although they are three individual chakras, their development builds on the foundation of the development of the previous chakra, so when the previous chakra is out of balance, it will likely have a direct effect on the subsequent chakras, and when the foundation of these three chakras is unstable, the health and wellness of the upper chakras is directly affected.

Root Chakra

Root Chakra Affirmation: I feel safe, strong, and grounded.

The root chakra is located at the base of the spine and is represented by the color red. The effects of the root chakra are most obvious between the ages of 0-7 years old. It is truly the root and foundation of your development.

Basic needs such as food, shelter, safety, comfort, and belonging affect our root chakra. When the root chakra is healthy and balanced, you may have a healthy physical body, feelings of strength, safety, and support in life. When the root chakra is unhealthy and imbalanced, you may have an unhealthy physical body, feelings of being unsafe, insecure, and unsupported in life.

Early childhood traumas usually set the stage for imbalanced root chakras. If you have had experiences or traumas in your childhood that have made you feel unsafe and that have gone without resolution, it is in your best interest to explore them, identify the belief systems gleaned from these situations, and the patterns developed by them and then work at reversing the momentum of these traumas one by one.

Some questions to ask yourself:

1. Do I feel safe?
2. What kind of things make me feel unsafe?
3. Am I safe in my environment and in my relationships? If not, why?
4. Do I feel strong and grounded?
5. Do I take care of my body?
6. Do I nourish it with healthy foods, physical activity, and do I spend time outdoors?

Because the root chakra is the foundation of your development, when it is imbalanced, it will adversely affect other aspects of your life.

To get a sense of how its imbalance affects your life, finish the following sentences:

1. When I don't feel safe, ...
2. When I don't feel strong, ...
3. When my body is not healthy, ...

If you find your root chakra is imbalanced, try to recall an early childhood memory that created feelings of being unsafe or insecure or lacking stability or grounding. Try to pinpoint the origin of the fear.

Ask yourself, what belief about myself or the world did I glean from this experience? Now go back to that experience and look at it from a logical, objective, adult's point of view and recognize that you are no longer that child, and release the fear attached to your experience. Become aware of how your childhood feelings of being unsafe, insecure, or unstable show themselves in your adult patterns. Keep this in your awareness and ask yourself in these moments, what new habits can I develop in order to promote a healthy root chakra?

There is are myriad of ways to bring balance to the root chakra, but first and foremost, address the source of the behavior that is creating the imbalance. In conjunction with addressing the "root" of the problem, certain foods, crystals, yoga, meditation, and healing music are beautiful and helpful supplements to creating balance in this area.

Sacral Chakra

Sacral Chakra Affirmation: I am radiant and beautiful. I lead a healthy and passionate life and am the creator of my entire reality.

The sacral chakra is located just below the navel. It is two inches into the pelvis and is represented by the color orange. The effects of the development of the sacral chakra are most obvious between the ages of 7-14 years old. Sexuality, the nature of relationships, freedom from guilt, pleasure, sensation, creativity, and the joys of life are affected by the functioning of the sacral chakra.

When the sacral chakra is balanced, you may have a healthy and respectable sex drive and may enjoy expressing yourself in creative ways that bring joy to yourself and others. You're likely to feel energetic and productive.

When the sacral chakra is imbalanced, you may feel disconnected from others sexually and have a lack of desire to be intimate with your partner. You're likely to feel sluggish, uncreative, and unproductive with no desire to make an effort with yourself, your personal needs, or your appearance.

Preadolescent and adolescent traumas usually set the stage for imbalanced sacral chakras. Similarly with the root chakra, if you have had experiences or traumas in your childhood that have gone without resolution, it is in your best interest to explore them, identify the belief systems gleaned from these situations and the patterns developed by them, and then to work at reversing the momentum of these traumas one by one.

When I personally take the time to examine the experiences from my formative years and look at my own chakra misalignments, I am able to glean such a deeper understanding of the causes of many of my unhealthy patterns that I've brought into adulthood. By doing this, I am able to reverse the trajectory of these patterns and increase the momentum with every decision and action that is for my best and highest good.

Bruno

When I examine my childhood experiences, I see a direct correlation between my unhealthy adulthood patterns and my sacral chakra. As for the root, I am generally an extremely grounded person. I haven't always been balanced, but I have always been grounded. When I look back at the "root years", I am able to recognize that although the energy was turbulent in my home, my needs were always met. I felt safe and comfortable. The men in my family (father, uncles, grandfather) were excellent provider types and exhibited characteristics of masculine strength and were quite financially secure. The women appeared to be outspoken, comfortable in their roles, and followed the rules of those roles. Clearly, things aren't always as they seem, but as a child between the ages of 0-7, this was how it appeared, so my basic needs were met, and I felt safe.

Somewhere around nine or ten years old, I began to feel the shift in my home. My parents' rocky relationship became more evident; my father left his career as an executive in NYC and was unemployed for several years. My brother and I were entering adolescence and developing our own opinions and perspectives on the world, and our home became an unbearable place to be.

As my brother was the elder, he was doted on by my mother which created part of the dynamic in our relationship, as he also learned through example the standing I had in my home. I handled my emotions with explosive behavior and histrionics, so I was often shut down with equal or greater force. My brother, with a more mild-mannered disposition, still shared the same parents and lived in the same environment, so on the outside, he smiled and accepted his circumstances, but he festered on the inside and took it out on me whenever he thought he could get away with it, which was often. As the home became more volatile, so did our relationship. This was the time when I began self-soothing with food, a coping mechanism that I utilized for most of my adult life.

After my father's departure from his job, he and my mother attempted to run a business together. My brother, from 6th-12th grade, attended a prestigious military school that included activities that kept him in school much later than me, leaving me at home unattended for many hours after school—just me, Chips Ahoy, and the remote control. I was young, but I remember in those moments, I felt the shame in knowing what I was doing, a feeling that stayed with me long into adulthood.

My parents' new business venture was relatively successful on a monetary level but led to their divorce when I was twelve years old, and like the marriage, the divorce was loud, aggressive, and ugly.

During these sacral years, the signs of my anger and depression became much more obvious: my weight fluctuated because of my binge eating and excessive dieting, my own volatility was evidenced in several fist fights in middle and even into high school, my grades, which were always straight A's, began to turn into mostly C's, and at twelve, I began smoking pot daily.

Yeah, I'd say the signs were there, but my parents didn't notice or appear to care. The adult Dana understands that they were both hurting so badly and immersed so deeply in their own personal dysfunction, trauma, and shame, that they were just unable to see past their own pain. The child Dana attached many irrational beliefs to this experience:

- *My needs do not matter.*
- *I am only really worthy of abuse and neglect.*
- *I must self-soothe because I cannot count on others for comfort.*
- *I must carry shame because my methods of self-soothing are shameful.*
- *And on some level, I am responsible for this upheaval because I am such a "difficult" child.*

When my father left our home, the consequences of my mother's inability to cope became evident in the volatile and often violent relationship between my brother and me. My brother was essentially let "off the chain" and was gifted me as his "whipping boy" as an outlet for his own coping with the dysfunction. I was just so lost and out of control with my own emotional imbalances, that finally, my father had to step in after about a year and a half to restore order.

According to my mother, she asked him for help because we were unmanageable, and she was on the verge of a nervous breakdown. She asked him to stay with us for a few days while she went away and got her head on straight, and he moved back in, in her words "lock, stock, and bag" and threatened that he'd kill her if she tried to return.

My father's story is that our mother abandoned us for another man, a man she met through my parents' business venture, who regardless of her denial, was very much in the picture. Likely, the truth fell somewhere between both of these "truths", but regardless of the real truth, the child's belief was:

- *I am not worthy of love because my own mother abandoned me.*
- *If I wasn't such a bad kid, my mother never would have left.*
- *My needs are never the priority.*

After living with my father and brother for the remainder of my 8th grade year, the summer I turned fourteen, the shit hit the fan. After having attempted to run away several times while essentially fleeing from conflict with my father, he and I had our final showdown, resulting in his taking my dog Bruno to the pound. My father drove me there, waited in the car, and sent me in with the dog, so I could release him to the authorities myself.

Sobbing, I walked in, put Bruno on the counter, and barely able to speak, I told them I was putting him up for adoption. They looked concerned, but didn't press, but they did inform me that the cost to relinquish my dog would be $25. I picked him up, brought him outside, still barely able to speak and informed my father of the cost.

He immediately stepped out of the car, dragged me inside, took a one-hundred-dollar bill out of his wallet, and slammed it on the counter. Then, he grabbed me by the arm and said, "Let's go."

As we were pulling away, a cop, who was called by the ladies inside, knocked at the window and asked if I was ok. My father replied, "She's fine." Then, the officer asked me if I was ok. With a pause, I then replied, "I'm fine," and we drove off without my dog.

Child's belief:
- *I am powerless.*
- *The people who love and care for me act in ways that aren't loving and caring.*

That was the day I ran away for good. After we returned

home and I had another brief confrontation with my father, I told him I was leaving, and for the first time, he didn't pursue, and I calmly walked out of my childhood home with only the clothes on my back.

That was the first day of more than two decades of estrangement with my father and my entire paternal family, including my grandmother, my aunts, my uncles, my cousins, everyone.

Several days later, once the dust had settled, I returned to pick up some of my things. When I approached the house, I was greeted with three black garbage bags on the front lawn. They were filled with whatever was in sight and within reach in my bedroom at the time. My entire life was reduced to three black garbage bags with my belongings sitting by themselves outside the house. I picked them up, put them in the car and left, never to reside in my childhood home again.

Child's belief:

- *I am garbage and should be treated as such.*

Obviously, there are so many more components that I could share about this story and what happened next, but what's important is the child's "take away" from the experience. Remember, I have mentioned four primary players in this story plus the ancillary players, and each one of them had a different perspective of what happened, why it happened, and the rights and wrongs of each player.

The reality is, however, that none of this matters. Child Dana's beliefs about myself and the world around me from the perspective of 10, 11, 12, 13, 14 are very real, and the patterns developed from these beliefs, gone unchecked, became the foundation of my identity and became concretized during the development of my solar plexus chakra and played out over and over throughout my life.

We all have our stories, but it's so important to not just tell your story, and to just remember that you had strife in your formative years, but to also ask yourself what you believe based on that strife and examine if it's a healthy belief system that reflects your highest good.

Some questions to ask yourself:
1. Do I feel I deserve the life I want?
2. Have I created a life that includes joy, passion, and creativity?
3. Do I complicate my life with too much mental activity?

4. How much pleasure do I feel I deserve each day?

5. Do I feel guilty when I allow myself to engage in pleasurable activities?

6. Do I like to be playful and try new activities?

7. Do I like to do fun things or go to fun places?

8. Do I enjoy creative activities?

9. Do I feel good about my body? If not, why?

10. What are some of my creative outlets?

11. Do I feel lethargic and disinterested in life?

12. Do I ever have feelings of depression?

Because the sacral chakra is the epicenter of your creativity, passion, and personal pleasure, when it is imbalanced, it will adversely affect other aspects of your life.

To get a sense of how its imbalance can affect your life, finish the following sentences:

1. If I feel lazy and unproductive, …

2. If I do not express my creativity, …

3. If I don't make an effort with myself or my appearance, …

Try this exercise:

1. Recall an unhappy or traumatic experience from preadolescence/adolescence.
2. Ask yourself, what belief about yourself or the world did you glean from this experience?
3. Is it rational, healthy, and in alignment with your highest good? Likely it's not.
4. What patterns have you created or experienced in your life based on this belief?
5. How does reliving this pattern make you feel?
6. Now go back to that experience and look at it from a logical, objective, adult's point of view and recognize that you are no longer that child.

Restructure your belief into a healthy, rational belief.

Ask yourself, what new habits can I develop in order to promote a healthy sacral chakra, and develop just one behavioral change that you can instill in your life that can help you reverse one of the patterns that you've created.

Once you are comfortable with this behavioral change, add another.

Rinse and repeat.

For years, I carried this story like a badge of honor,

knowing it played an integral part in shaping me and my character, making me the "tough girl", an identity I perfected during the development of my solar plexus chakra, but for many years, I hadn't truly understood the impact of this experience.

I had gleaned many irrational beliefs from this experience. As a result, patterns of abuse, neglect, and unworthiness repeated over and over in my life, but upon reflection, having done the work, having released the pain of the emotional attachment and the child's beliefs, I was able to truly identify the gifts.

My ability to release attachments to things, relationships, and situations that no longer serve me was birthed during this era of my life, offering me great moments of peace later in life.

The independence that I was forced to draw on over and over and over in my life established itself during this trauma, allowing me to overcome enormous obstacles with very little support over the years to come.

My adaptability, which began as a seedling during this crisis, was practiced throughout my life experience and became one of my most valuable tools for survival.

Most importantly, I learned forgiveness and compassion. I've learned that my darkest times have offered the most beautiful gifts, and when I release the judgement of myself and others, exercise compassion for all that are involved, and forgive, the gifts are endless, and the beauty of these experiences becomes inescapable.

Solar Plexus Chakra

Solar Plexus Affirmation: I am worthy of and empowered to pursue my purpose.

The solar plexus chakra is located directly below the sternum above the stomach and is represented by the color yellow. The effects of the solar plexus chakra are most obvious between the ages of 14-21 years old. The solar plexus is the center of personal identity. It rules all aspects of our personality and ego. This includes our sense of self-worth, self-esteem, and personal identity.

When the solar plexus chakra is healthy and balanced, you may have a strong healthy will and a strong healthy sense of personal power. You tend to think highly of the person you are and the ability that you have to be successful and abundant in all areas of your life. You are likely motivated and pursue your goals in a healthy and proactive way which brings you joy, success, and personal fulfillment.

When the solar plexus chakra is unhealthy and imbalanced, you may have low self-esteem, and you often base your self-worth on the opinions of others. You are likely insecure and lack confidence in your ability to accomplish your goals and dreams. You may seek and need recognition from others to feel appreciated and often feel powerless to build the life that you desire and often settle for less than you deserve, leaving you unmotivated and unfulfilled.

Adolescent and young adult experiences and traumas as well as the weak foundation of misaligned root and sacral chakras usually set the stage for imbalanced solar plexus chakras. If you have had experiences or traumas in your childhood that have gone without resolution, it is in your best interest to explore them, identify the belief systems gleaned from these situations, and the patterns developed by them and then to work at reversing the momentum of these traumas one by one.

Some questions to ask yourself:
1. How strongly do I value myself?
2. Do I see worth in others who do not see their own light shining?
3. Do I see my own?

4. What do I consider the kindest thing I have ever done for others?

5. What do I consider the kindest thing I have ever done for myself?

6. Do I know that I am always free to choose in every situation?

7. Am I confident that I will succeed in my tasks and with the things that are important to me?

Because the solar plexus chakra is the center of your empowerment and personal identity, when it is imbalanced, it will adversely affect other aspects of your life.

To get a sense of how its imbalance affects your life, finish the following sentences:

1. When my self-worth depends on the opinions of others, …

2. When I am insecure about my abilities, …

3. When I fear failure, …

As with the root and sacral chakras, it is important to identify the source of the imbalance that occurred during the years of resonance (in the case of the solar plexus, 14-21 years) and work through the steps of reversing the attached belief systems that no longer serve you. Then ask yourself, what new habits can I develop in order to promote a healthy solar plexus chakra? This is a process that will bring you peace and alignment in all areas of your life and with time and attention will become second nature to you.

As a result of my personal trauma during the development of my sacral chakra, I entered the years of my solar plexus development having to overcome many obstacles for survival. For the next several years, my family life was imbalanced, my household structure was unstable, and my educational structure and routine had been uprooted and difficult to stabilize. I was emotionally in pain, and my needs were neglected. My identity was developed around my need for survival and "Tough Girl Dana" became my personal identity.

My newest belief system became: *Life is hard, but I am strong, and I will overcome all obstacles.*

It is important to remember that nothing in life lives in a vacuum—everything is interconnected, including the chakra system—and when one of them is out of balance, specifically in the foundation, other chakras and other areas of your life can be adversely affected.

Although all the chakras exist from the time of birth,

like I mentioned, their major stage of resonance develops with the child, and when the child becomes stunted by the former chakra(s), the latter chakras do not reach their full potential with their energetic resonance.

In the simplest terms, when the foundation of the first three chakras is faulty, the next four chakras develop as follows:

The heart chakra, which encompasses your ability to love in a healthy manner, becomes imbalanced because the child's coping mechanisms to protect the heart and its foundation is based on fear.

The throat chakra, which encompasses your ability to speak and live authentically, becomes imbalanced, because its foundation is also based on fear. Also, to truly live authentically, you must have an open heart.

The third eye and crown chakras encompass your ability to connect with your inner wisdom, trust your intuition, and tap into the universal love and wisdom that is available to all. Both of these chakras depend entirely on the health of the previous chakras to be able to function to their full potential.

In essence, we all have the magic within us. We all are born with love, truth, intuition, and connectedness, but

when our foundation becomes cracked through the trauma of our experiences, our magic becomes buried in the rubble. Once we understand this and repair, restructure, and in some cases, rebuild our foundation, we reveal a whole new layer of ourselves, and life truly begins to become magical.

Heart Chakra

Heart Chakra Affirmation: I am love. I am open to receive love. I give love freely without condition or expectation.

The purpose of the heart chakra is love, compassion, and forgiveness and is represented by the color green. When the heart chakra is healthy and balanced, you may be able to be kind, loving, and compassionate towards others and have healthy, respectful, win-win relationships. You are likely to have healthy self-esteem, and you can say that you truly love, respect and appreciate the person you are! You are able to deal with loss in a healthy way, and you allow yourself to forgive not only yourself but others as well.

When the heart chakra is unhealthy and imbalanced, you may behave unkindly and disrespectfully towards others, and you tend to attract people who can be unloving and disrespectful toward you. You are likely in an unhealthy, imbalanced relationship and are less than joyful most of the time. You probably don't much care for the person you are and tend to experience more negative emotions than loving and positive emotions. You don't deal with disappointment or loss very well and tend to hold grudges for those who have "wronged" you in the past.

Some questions to ask yourself:
1. Do I feel loved?
2. Do I give love?
3. How do I show love?
4. When do I feel the most loved?
5. When do I feel unloved?
6. Do I love myself as readily as I can love others?
7. Do I readily forgive others?
8. Do I forgive myself?
9. Do I love without condition or expectation?
10. In what ways am I protecting my heart chakra?

Because the heart chakra is the epicenter of your ability to love and be loved, when it is imbalanced, it will adversely affect other aspects of your life.

To get a sense of how its imbalance affects your life, finish the following sentences:

1. When I am feeling unloved, …
2. When I love another with an expectation, …
3. When I make choices that do not reflect love or care for myself, …

Ask yourself, what new habits can I develop in order to promote a healthy heart chakra?

Throat Chakra

Throat Chakra Affirmation: I am honest with myself and others and speak and live authentically.

The throat chakra is located in your internal and external throat and is represented by the color blue. This chakra is directly linked to your personal integrity and sense of honor. The gift of this chakra is accepting your originality, expressing your authentic voice, and speaking your truth which is based and anchored in your heart chakra.

When the throat chakra is healthy and balanced, it allows you to communicate well with others and handle conflict with respect and honesty. You'll notice that people respect you and speak to you in a way that is kind and appropriate. You have no problem expressing your true feelings, thoughts, ideas, and creativity in a healthy way. You are a good listener and allow others to express themselves in a healthy and respectful way when they are around you.

When the throat chakra is unhealthy and imbalanced, you have the inability to communicate well with others, and you might have difficulty expressing clear and appropriate boundaries for yourself. You tend to hold in your true feelings and often don't voice your own ideas or opinions. You may yell at others and speak to others in a disrespectful way and tend to gossip. You also may not be the best listener when others are trying to communicate with you.

Some questions to ask yourself:

1. Do I express my feelings with ease?
2. Am I comfortable setting boundaries for myself?

3. Do I feel heard when I speak with others?

4. Are my words and actions in alignment with each other?

5. Am I being honest with myself?

6. Am I honest with others?

7. What does it mean to speak my truth?

8. Am I living authentically?

Because the throat chakra is directly linked to your personal sense of integrity and authenticity, when it is imbalanced, it will adversely affect other aspects of your life.

To get a sense of how its imbalance affects your life, finish the following sentences:

1. When I don't feel heard, …

2. When my words don't match my actions, …

3. When I am not honest with myself or others, …

Ask yourself, what new habits can I develop in order to promote a healthy throat chakra?

Third Eye Chakra

Third Eye Chakra Affirmation: I embrace my imagination and trust my intuition.

The third eye chakra is located between the eyebrows and is represented by the color indigo or purple and is responsible for imagination, psychic abilities, your sense of purpose, self-reflection, visualization, discernment, and trust of your own intuition.

When the third eye chakra is healthy and balanced, it presents in your ability to see the beauty in the world, and you tend to be someone who tries to find the opportunity and positivity in all situations and the good in all people. You likely trust your intuition and let it guide you when appropriate. You allow yourself to be a dreamer and are open to the possibility of your dreams materializing in your life. You are able to see and honor the light that is within yourself and also see and honor the light that is within others.

When the third eye chakra is unhealthy and im-balanced, you may be unable to recognize patterns (of life situations and events). You may lack the ability to focus on tasks and goals and potentially develop obsessive behaviors. You may also tend to ignore your intuitive nudges and ignore opportunities to be imaginative.

Some questions to ask yourself:
1. Am I imaginative?
2. Do I listen to my intuition?
3. How does my intuition speak to me?
4. When my intuition speaks to me, do I ignore it?
5. How do I discern who and what is for my greatest benefit?
6. Using my own wisdom, can I forgive the past and extract the learning that was there for me?
7. Am I able to detect patterns and see the big picture to discern what's the best course of action for my highest good?

Because the third eye chakra is directly linked to your intuition and inner wisdom, when it is imbalanced, it will adversely affect other aspects of your life.

To get a sense of how its imbalance affects your life, finish the following sentences:
1. If I don't allow myself to use my imagination, ...
2. If I am unable to see patterns in people's behavior

or events, …

3. If I ignore my body's natural guidance system, …

Ask yourself, what new habits can I develop in order to promote a healthy third eye chakra?

Crown Chakra

Crown Chakra Affirmation: I am in connection with my spirit and trust my intuition.

The crown chakra is located on top of the head and is represented by the color violet or white. The gift of the crown chakra is experiencing unity and the selfless realization that everything is connected at a fundamental level.

When the crown chakra is balanced, you may have a strong connection to universal wisdom and support that exists at least partially somewhere outside of yourself. You believe in the love and support of this creative source and are open to receiving love, guidance, and inspiration from this source.

When the crown chakra is imbalanced, you may have very little activity within this chakra, but areas where you may notice issues are in your limited beliefs, and you may find it difficult to understand or respect the beliefs of others. You may experience feelings of depression, addictive behaviors, feelings of apathy, chronic worrying, and chronic exhaustion.

Some questions to ask yourself:

1. Can I create the time I need to be still and connect with nature?
2. Do I feel I can be loved, healed, and cherished by simply being myself?
3. Do I feel connected to the ultimate reality?
4. What does taking care of my spirit look like?
5. When I am taking care of my spirit, how does it bleed into other aspects of my life?

Because the crown chakra is directly linked to your intuition and connection to universal love and wisdom, when it is imbalanced, it will adversely affect other aspects of your life.

To get a sense of how its imbalance affects your life, finish the following sentences:

1. When I worry, ...
2. When I don't care about things, ...
3. When I'm tired all the time, ...

Ask yourself: what new habits can I develop in order to promote a healthy crown chakra?

Addressing Physical Maladies

When your energy centers are healthy, the correlating aspects of your life generally run properly and smoothly. When your energy centers are imbalanced, dysfunction in these areas begins to appear. It's also important to note that when a chakra is not properly functioning or if it is blocked, maladies can form in these areas and illness can possibly occur, so strengthening and enhancing the flow in your chakra areas is crucial to your emotional and physical health.

Over the last few decades, I have had a few health crises that upon further examination, have directly correlated to my misaligned chakras. At the time, I was unaware of the energetic influence on my physical health and treated my maladies through traditional medicine. However, I presently address my residual conditions through a holistic approach, utilizing my understanding of the chakra system. While, over the years, I had been diagnosed with Barrett's Esophagitis, Rheumatoid Arthritis, Thyroid Carcinoma, and have been riddled with uterine cysts and fibroid tumors for most of my adult life, I no longer take any medication. None. Nada. Zilch. Seriously, nothing. I understand, based on our collective belief systems about medicine, that this is difficult to believe, but it is true and will be further discussed in the Eighth Recommandment.

Here's the real beauty of this guidance system. If you are out of alignment in a certain area of your life, you can likely trace it back to one of these energy centers. Then you can dissect the reason for the imbalance, and then you can remedy it. When imbalances are addressed in real time, not allowing for the momentum of years of misalignment to kick in, the chakras are much easier to bring into balance without the consequences manifesting into serious life altering consequences or physical maladies. When imbalances are ignored, not only are the consequences far greater but the reversal of the momentum can be a more challenging process to overcome. This is why tending to the health of your chakras is integral for personal wellness, *and* not to mention, they are color coded! How cool is that?!

Fifth Recommandment

I shalt not settle for anything less than my general contentment.

Rather, I SHALL recognize and understand that my most natural state of being is to always be in a state of general contentment, and when I'm not, it's always in my best interest to begin taking the steps toward contentment—one at a time, asking myself "What do I need in this moment?"

I truly believe that our purpose in this world is for personal growth and expansion and to experience joy and love while doing so. I also believe that our natural state of being is always to be content, and if we are not content, we have a personal obligation to figure out what is causing the discontent, and through our own actions, transmute it into contentment. If this is a difficult concept to embrace, take a few moments and observe children when their needs are being met.

When children feel safe and secure in their environment, they only experience the joy and wonder of that experience in that moment of time. Whether it's chasing a butterfly or staring at a blade of grass or running and spinning just for the sake of running or spinning, the child resides in that moment and exudes only joy in that moment. When something occurs to disrupt their joy that makes them feel unsafe or as if their needs aren't being met, only then do they begin to apply their coping mechanisms to return to their most comfortable state—JOY.

If our most natural state of being is truly contentment, and we are not feeling content, then it would behoove us, in that moment, to take the most available and appropriate step(s) toward contentment. Right?

Ask yourself NOT What am I *supposed* to do?

Ask yourself NOT what do I *have* to do?

Ask yourself what do I *feel* like doing?

We convince ourselves that so many other pressing or important things in our lives trump contentment, but this is a misconception. First, we must take care of our own wellbeing, and then everything else not only falls into place but also does so with much more ease, creating more contentment.

For children, this process is generally simple. They do what they want when they want, sometimes regardless of an adverse consequence, and most children bounce back relatively quickly from adversity.

A child is running on the playground and stumbles and falls. If there is no adult fear-based intervention, the child will get up and continue running. If an injury is involved, the child will seek to have their needs met and then will continue onto what brings them joy—running.

For adults, this process often becomes a little more complicated and convoluted because of the beliefs, patterns, and behaviors that have accumulated over the years. If we stumble and fall on the playground, we have learned to expect an outcome, instilling fear. If the injury is minor, we have learned to dwell on all of the potential outcomes of that fall, instilling fear. We have learned to attach blame to the fall. We have learned judgement which results in embarrassment about the fall. In essence, our expectation, attachment, and judgement of our fall on the playground inhibits our ability to return to joy in the same way a child does.

With that said, it makes total sense that if a child doesn't know to be fearful, they won't carry the same amount and kind of "baggage" as an adult who has had many previous experiences that have elicited fear. However, with an awareness of our fears and a willingness to decipher between rational and irrational fears, we can have a healthy relationship with our experiences and a more enjoyable life.

As I mentioned earlier, when a child feels discontented,

they will attempt to have their needs met, applying the age-appropriate skills that they have learned up until that point. As adults, when we find ourselves discontented, we tend to ignore this signal from our emotional guidance system that is telling us a tweak or change needs to be made. Rather, we often accept this state of being, deny it, place blame for it, or mask it with some form of distraction or "self-medication" of sorts.

If I am feeling discontent, I have some choices:

1. **I can ignore my feelings altogether, but I'm pretty sure we all know how that turns out.**

   Usually, resentment follows or an exacerbation of the initial cause of the discontent.

2. **I can become mired in the emotion and blame the catalyst (person, event, or both) for the experience, never taking responsibility for my own experience.** As a result, I will never work through the problem and never achieve a resolution.

3. **I can recognize that I'm not in a state of contentment and make a choice to feel better and choose a momentary "salve" for my discomfort.** I may eat a cookie. That always makes me feel better (for the moment). I may have a drink or smoke something or buy something, all things that

satisfy the emotional discontentment signal momentarily. The reality, however, is that if I'm receiving the signal and I put it on "snooze", at some point, the signal will return, and in these cases, it gets louder and less comfortable.

4. **I can recognize that I'm not in a state of contentment and make a choice to feel better by identifying the source of discontent and addressing it at the source.**

A good practice to gauge contentment is to ask yourself, **"How am I feeling in this moment?" or "Do I have everything I need to feel content in this moment?"**

If the answer is no, it is very important to ask the following questions:

- **"What step(s) can I take in this moment to move closer to contentment?"**
- **"What can I do right NOW to feel better in this moment?"**

These questions are so important because we have a tendency to become so overwhelmed with our busy lives or the complexity of our problems that the process of self-improvement paralyzes us sometimes, but the truth is we only have this moment and when we address our discontent one moment at a time, anything is possible.

If I am deciding to end an unhappy relationship that requires me to change my place of residence, I may feel overwhelmed at the prospect of doing this and stay far longer than what's in my highest good. I am more inclined to "self-medicate" my discontent with food, drink, smoke, and entertainment than to address the matter at hand because of my overwhelming feelings.

However, if I ask myself, **"What step(s) can I take in this moment to move closer to contentment?"** I may be less likely to become paralyzed by the overwhelming feeling of what's next.

"What can I do right NOW to feel better in this moment?"

1. Well, I can create clear boundaries in the house.
2. I can express with respect and clarity what I need from my partner to feel more comfortable in the house.
3. I can look for alternative living arrangements and begin making an exit plan.

By focusing on what you can do in this moment not only shifts the focus onto this moment, but it also puts the power into your hands, alleviating the feelings of anxiety and discontentment.

The following example is going to sound very basic and very silly, but this practice has been a game changer in my life. Because I have always been a bit of a bulldozer that pushes past obstacles, rather than acquiesce until the proper door opens, I have always treated everything like the Kool-Aid guy, plowing through walls regardless of the consequence. I blew through life rather quickly, and many times got what I wanted and accomplished what I needed, but I often ignored the details that mattered for a more sensory driven, fulfilling life.

I spilled more, I burned my tongue more, I bumped into things more, and I ignored many of my basic needs. Everything I did was with speed and intensity, often resulting in a missed experience or in discomfort of some sort. I was always moving onto the next thing, having experienced my present situation at 80% fulfillment.

I prided myself on being a powerhouse that "got shit done", but I wouldn't go for a pedicure because it took too long, or if I did go, I would skip the foot massage part because "what's the point? I've got shit to do!"

Only recently, because I have had some medical issues (that I discuss in the Eighth Recommandment), have I forced myself to slow down, and in doing so, I have truly comprehended my disservice to myself throughout all of those years.

The first time I put the questions **"How am I feeling in this moment?"** and **"What can I do right NOW to feel better in this moment?"** into practice, I was amazed by what I experienced.

As a means to slow down and allow my body to heal, I decided to spend twenty minutes every morning sitting outside—no music, no phone, no technology, no distractions.

Day 1, I went outside on my back deck, sat on an Adirondack chair, kicked my feet up on the fire pit, and stared at the preserve behind my house. I was fine but ready to pop out of that chair in 20 minutes flat!

After a moment, I asked myself,

"How am I feeling in this moment?"

Well, I'm a little chilly (something I would have ignored before).

"What can I do right NOW to feel better in this moment?"

I can get a blanket (something I wouldn't have done before).

So, I got up to get a blanket and asked myself, **"What**

else can I do right NOW to feel better in this moment?"

I can really go for a cup of coffee.

After a few minutes, I returned outside, wrapped in a blanky with a hot cup of coffee in my hand ready to sit. After a moment, I asked myself,

"How am I feeling in this moment?"

Still a little chilly.

"What can I do right NOW to feel better in this moment?"

I then moved my legs that were actually feeling uncomfortable and adjusted the blanket so my legs were covered. After a few moments, I asked myself,

"How am I feeling in this moment?"

Much to my surprise, I was feeling so comfortable, so much at peace and so content. All my needs were met, and I took so much joy from the experience of just sitting in nature with a cup of coffee staring at trees. By the time my 20 minutes was over, I was like a big, gooey, joy blob. It was truly something!

My take away from this experience was how infrequently we check in with ourselves about our own personal needs and general contentment. Somewhere along the line, during the hustle and bustle of our lives, we've come to accept discontent as a general way of being on both a physical and emotional level, and when this discomfort evolves into pain, unhappiness, depression, or physical maladies, we then take notice. By that time, the magnitude of our personal neglect either feels like a hopeless situation to address or we feel we are powerless and must seek assistance outwardly, for example, through doctors, therapists, and prescriptions. However, in reality, if we just take the time to check in with ourselves, we will come to realize the power is in OUR hands.

Since that day, I have made a point to ask myself those questions as often as I can. Initially, this practice may require diligence, sometimes even on a moment-to-moment basis, but as it becomes a habit and ultimately a way of being, the awareness of how you're feeling and what you need to do to return to contentment becomes second nature.

Again, our most natural state of being is to always be in a state of general contentment, and when we're not, it's always in our best interest to begin taking the steps toward contentment—one at a time, step by step, and you will witness yourself creating your own beautiful existence right before your very eyes.

Sixth Recommandment

I shalt not judge, attach, or expect anything from anyone or any situation.

Rather, I SHALL recognize and under-stand that judgement, attachment, and expectation rob me of my peace.

A very wise friend once said to me that she is living in her most natural state of being and wholeness (or contentment) when she is experiencing peace, joy, and love and that when she is NOT experiencing peace, joy and love, it's because she is experiencing, on some level, judgement, attachment, or expectation. This statement resonated with me so deeply that I took some time to examine the veracity of the statement. Although these behaviors are often intertwined and often occur concurrently, I am going to explain them each individually.

Judgement

Judgement is tricky because for our survival, we must hone the ability to exercise discernment in all situations. It is our discernment that informs us of what best serves us. When emotions and even attachment and expectation become enmeshed with discernment, this can lead to judgement, thus robbing us of peace.

When I left my career in education in 2017, my family and I moved into a more affordable house in a rural area in Jupiter, Florida, so as a family, we could afford to live on a single salary. This would allow us to have more land and more privacy, and the children would experience a safer and more natural environment.

The property was 1.25 acres and just beautiful! In the three and a half years that we resided in Jupiter Farms, we were front row center to nature in all its glory. We encountered a plethora of wild animals, from lizards, frogs, snakes to moles, turtles, bunnies to bobcats, boars, coyotes, and birds, and my God, the variety of birds was endless. The sandhill cranes and hawks were my absolute favorite. Just so magnificent!

I once even watched a bobcat skulking through the neighbors' yard with one of their chickens in his mouth in the middle of the afternoon! To which I heard myself mutter, "What the f@*&%! am I looking at?!"

During this time, I had also experienced many of what I would consider tragedies on my own property. During our first spring in The Farms, my nine-year-old had a cardinal nest right outside her window. When she found it, it just held eggs. Then we were alerted to the babies' arrival by the chirps, and every day, we would all peer through the window and watch them and listen to their little chirps, until one day, my daughter's blood curdling screams alerted me to the snake that was eating one of the baby birds. Even typing this hurts my heart a little bit.

I immediately reacted also by screaming like a freaking lunatic, of course, and in a panic enlisted my husband to help stop this evil act of terror. I then ran outside and began throwing anything I could get my hands on at the snake, including one of my potted plants. My husband, only trying to placate his wife who was completely out of her mind got a shovel and killed the snake, something that still weighs heavily on both our hearts. In my initial judgement of the situation, the baby birds were innocent, the snake was a murderer, and I was the savior of all the baby animals. My attachment to the birds and my expectation of how things "should" be certainly didn't help the situation.

As much as I would love to say that this was the only experience of its kind, I would be lying. In the three and a half years that we lived in that house, the number of bunnies, lizards, and mice that I pulled out of the clutches of my own house cat is staggering, the whole time resenting the family cat for being a dirty murderer.

I cannot even begin to express how traumatic these

experiences were for me and my family. In retrospect, however, it was MY judgement of the behaviors of what I deemed "murderous animals" was what robbed me of my peace. You see, in the natural world, there is no judgement of good and evil, just the acknowledgement of imbalance resulting in the restoration of balance. There are no victims or victors, just predators and prey. All living things have their natural cycles, patterns, and behaviors, and they do what they do in accordance with that.

Nature's sense of restoring balance is an important lesson for us. When humans are imbalanced, we tend to put a judgement on it that in many cases includes fear, shame, guilt, and anger.

For many years, I battled with my own anger. Since I was a little girl, when triggered by fear, my "fight or flight" response was always, I mean ALWAYS, fight. I grew up with so much shame and guilt about it because I created situations in which I was judged as bad, or mean, or even beastly.

I shamefully judged myself as well, but the reality was, my emotional response to fear induced situations was imbalanced. Period. Once I learned how to balance my fear response, my anger dissipated. As a society, we are conditioned to place judgement on things, especially ourselves. This perspective not only separates humanity, but when the judgement is placed on ourselves, it keeps us living in shame and guilt, ultimately robbing us of the peace that we are craving.

How do we release our judgements?

1. Recognize that everything that we perceive is just information. That is all. Our response to that information is just a signal to us about what serves us best.

If someone offered me two ice cream cones, vanilla and chocolate, and offered me the choice between the two, I would choose based on my previous experience with those flavors.

I would remember that I preferred chocolate to vanilla based on how I felt when I previously tasted chocolate, and I would choose chocolate.

I would not judge the inferiority of the vanilla. I would not renounce vanilla by mentioning all the times I was disappointed by the flavor. I would not go on social media and talk trash about how evil vanilla is and try to convince others to feel the same.

I would use the information that I received through my earlier experiences with vanilla to help guide me to the flavor I preferred and eat my ice cream in peace.

2. There is no #2. It is all just information.

In March 2021, in honor of my first published book, *Veda Finds Her Crown,* Ubuntu Fish Gallery hosted Chakra-Con—a book launching, book signing, and celebration of the health and education of our chakras for personal empowerment. It was a very exciting time for me because I both wrote and illustrated this book and had been planning for this event for months prior.

Unfortunately, another friend of mine was having an event on the same day about an hour away that was equally as important and exciting for her. We realized there was a conflict about a month prior, commiserated about it, and moved on with our lives.

A few days prior to our events, when I texted her to offer her my best wishes for her event, she responded with shock and anger that I was not going, accusing me of being a shitty and selfish friend and also reminding me of what a good friend she had been to me. Obviously, my initial emotional response was to feel anger, defensiveness, and the need to respond in kind. Instead, I took a breath and looked at the information that was being presented.

1. This person was unable to see past her needs to also see my needs.

2. This person lashed out at me the moment she didn't get what she wanted from me.

3. After processing her accusations, I understood that my perspective of my friendship with her differed from *her* perspective of my friendship with her.

4. Looking back, I saw a pattern of behavior from her that included similar accusations with the same vehement delivery.

5. If I was being honest with myself, there had been some dissonance developing for some time.

Objectively looking at this information helped me release the initial anger and defensiveness, thwarting an explosive response back at her. I asked myself based on the information, if this relationship still served me. The answer was *no*. The relationship is over. How did I respond, you ask? I didn't.

Expectation

Expectation, much like judgement, is often a difficult line to tow. Decisions that are in our best interest require discernment, but when emotion is attached, discernment, what's in my best and highest good, becomes judgement, what's right or wrong, and it strips us of our peace. Similarly, intention is important for creating the lives we desire, but when attachment becomes a part of the equation, intention becomes expectation, setting us up for disappointment and often heartache. In order to truly avoid expectation, we must be honest about our intentions.

I am a pretty generous person by nature, and I have always been generous with my time, my energy, my money, my stuff, my food, pretty much everything. Giving of myself is the best expression of my ability to share love, and I truly believed my intentions were pure. Although my generosity is relatively universal, with my willingness to give to acquaintances, colleagues, and even strangers, I have been especially generous with my more intimate relationships, especially the romantic ones. I suppose the more intimate the relationship, the deeper the love, the greater capacity to give. Makes sense, I suppose.

When I review many of my romantic relationships as

well as a few platonic relationships, I find one commonality. I almost always, and I am being conservative by using the word *almost,* walked away feeling like my generosity was not reciprocated. The irony is that the less I received, the more I gave, and the more disappointed I became, the more I ended up giving. I can't even begin to count the thousands of dollars that I have gifted, loaned, or felt swindled out of over the years under the guise of love.

These love stories always ended the same way—*I don't understand. I did everything I could do for this person, only to be taken for a fool.* The more heartache I experienced and the larger the loss, the more I invested in the subsequent relationship. I truly believed my generosity was unappreciated, and I was just a giver, and these people were all takers. In other words, I was "victimized" by other people's lack of regard for my needs. This was truly a pattern that I had perfected!

Let's break this down:

1. I became the victim in all of these situations because I acted as if something had been done to me, when in reality, I created the pattern, perpetuated the pattern, and perfected the pattern of unreciprocated love.

2. I created this pattern based on my belief system that I am not worthy of love and that I must overcompensate in order to be loved in return.

3. I did not love unconditionally; rather, I loved with expectation. If I give everything I have to give, then on some level, that person would be obligated to love me back.

My expectation of a return on my love investment was not only a direct reflection of my deep feelings of unworthiness, but it also kept me from the one thing that I craved the most—LOVE.

Is loving someone with a level of expectation really love or is it a way of manipulating the situation to get unfulfilled needs met?

For me, for most of my life, it was truly the only way I knew how to love, and I "loved" under the guise of generosity when in reality it was desperation.

However, throughout my own personal evolution, I learned how to love—how to love without any expectation attached to it. Through my own personal experiences and insights, I learned that love is not necessarily about doing or giving, it's about being. As I progressed in my personal development and committed acts of self-love and self-care by looking at myself, my behaviors, my patterns, and accepting personal accountability for my life and my decisions, and when I stopped blaming others and embraced the opportunity for growth in both the pleasant and unpleasant circumstances, I began to understand love on a whole other level. Once I understood that fear and love do not reside in the same place, I began to understand that all of the choices I made "in the name of love" were actually in the name of desperation and unworthiness that were deeply rooted in fear.

Once I learned how to love without fear and without expectation, love came to me far more readily, and the interesting part is, as a result, I became a far more generous person because the giving of my time, my energy, my money, my stuff, my food, pretty much everything no longer came with an expectation but rather true unconditional love.

Navigating the difference in extremes is a delicate dance, but once we become aware of the differences and adapt this awareness to our daily practices, we will find that the joy, peace, and love will return, leading us to our freedom.

Attachment

It is in our human nature to attach to things. The level of attachment varies from person to person and from thing to thing, but regardless of the attachment, the one common denominator is that our attachments are based in fear, and when we attach ourselves to money, status, material possessions, identity, outcomes, and relationships, we ultimately rob ourselves of the peace and freedom that we desire.

Special Edition! Mini recommandment within the recommandment—for the sake of organization, we'll call it:

Recommandment 6 A
I shalt not become a prisoner of my own desires.

Rather, I SHALL recognize that all I truly want is peace and freedom. I understand that peace and freedom are unique and personal

and to attain these states of being, I must first identify what peace and freedom look like to me, identify the steps to get there, and take them.

Also, I understand that desiring a life that brings me joy and contentment is not a crime, and desiring cool things, interesting relationships and exciting experiences that add to that joy and contentment is not a crime. Attaching to those desires, those relationships, those things, and those experiences is still not a crime, but attaching to them is and will always be contradictory to my desire for peace and freedom.

Attachment to "Stuff"

Unexamined attachments are sometimes difficult to detect, and most people don't even realize all the attachments that they carry. The most obvious form of attachment, I believe, is the attachment to "stuff". We, as a human race, acquire stuff to which we attach meaning.

Sometimes it carries a personal meaning: *This once belonged to my…who I loved so very much, so it is very important that I have it, hold it, cherish it, protect it and if something happens to it, mourn it.*

In most cases, however, we acquire stuff that gives us a feeling of safety or freedom—house, car, monetary acquisitions, etc. We acquire stuff that makes us feel sexy or confident—clothing, recreational accouterments, cars, boats, electronics, toiletries. Essentially, we acquire stuff that makes us feel freedom—freedom from fear, lack, or insecurity.

We believe that when we surround ourselves with stuff that makes us feel safe or free, or when it even reminds us of love, then we will finally find contentment. The reality is that the stuff that was intended to bring feelings of security, freedom, or love have quite the opposite effect.

When we attach our well-being to stuff, we are no longer empowered to create our own feelings of security, freedom, or love. We rely on external acquisitions to ignite those feelings in us, and when we spend our lives in pursuit and protection of those acquisitions, we not only rob ourselves of joy, but we also imprison ourselves, ultimately robbing ourselves of the freedom we seek.

As a general rule, I try to purge the stuff that no longer serves me every six months to a year. I find the decluttering helps with my mental organization. Additionally, when my children or I bring something new into the house, generally new clothes or toys, I (we) take the time to go through our things and donate what no longer serves us.

I have taught my children to make three piles:

1. I absolutely can't live without/use on a daily basis.
2. I don't really use or need, but I am not sure I want to let it go.
3. Toss this. I didn't even know I still had it.

What usually happens is pile #1 and #3 are usually very small, and pile #2 requires some attention. The purpose of this exercise is to teach my children (and myself, of course) to constantly take inventory of our possessions, and to recognize the attachment and to let go of the stuff that no longer serves them.

Initially, this practice is challenging because the fear and attachment seeps in.

"But what if someday I need this pair of dull scissors that I never use?"

"But I got this (plastic piece of crap) at the zoo in the

2nd grade on my class trip and it's special."

What they must come to realize is the attachment to the thing that connects them to the memory is no longer necessary because that memory is now a part of them, and when memories are processed in a healthy manner, having "stuff" only gets in the way.

The Trunk

Over the years, I have moved quite a bit. I grew up in New Jersey, attended college in Florida, and have explored several cities in Florida over the last thirty years before now settling in Stuart.

When I was in my late twenties, and the writing was on the wall that I would probably not be returning to New Jersey, my mother shrink wrapped an old trunk filled with memories from my high school and college years and shipped it to Florida, so I would have it. Knowing there was nothing in it that I needed, I put it deep in my closet, out of the way.

Since I received that trunk, I have moved three times. Each time, still shrink wrapped, that trunk would get put deep into another closet, out of the way.

During this most recent move, about a year or so ago,

my husband finally asked me what was in the trunk, and to be honest, I didn't even know, but for some reason I had some trepidation about going in there. After completely moving into my house, I knew that trunk was next. I circled it for a week or so until I finally committed to sitting down and going through everything.

Oh my goodness, what I found! So many memories! So many things forgotten! People forgotten! Experiences forgotten! Letters! Oh my God, the letters! Letters from "loves" that I couldn't even remember. Pictures of people I no longer recognized. Mementos from travels abroad. I went through everything, had some laughs, felt the emotion, processed it, let it go, and I then put it in a pile. I spent over an hour going through everything. Then I saw what I knew on some level was in there, the reminder of a love lost when I was twenty-one years old—a boyfriend with whom I had a beautiful romance during a summer I spent in Italy. I found letters, pictures, and even the letter his sister sent with a Mass card and picture to inform me of his death.

In that moment, I realized that I never properly grieved his passing, that I locked away my grief like I did this trunk. In that moment, as I opened that trunk, I opened my heart and allowed myself to properly grieve. There I was, sitting on the floor of my closet, surrounded by thirty-year-old memories, face in hands, sobbing for that twenty-one-year-old girl that had her heart broken so terribly so long ago.

In that moment, I understood so much about how stifling that experience, denying my trauma and muscling through, shaped my relationships and my "ability" to love in the years to come. I then took a few breaths, wiped my tears, put everything back in the trunk except for three or four miscellaneous items, closed the clasps, and prepared to ask my husband to bring the trunk out to the curb.

As I exited my closet, I turned around, opened the trunk, retrieved that one final picture of Vincenzo, put it in a drawer, closed it up and proceeded to ask for my husband's assistance.

As difficult and as bold as that whole exercise of letting go was, I was still not ready to let go of that one picture, and that's OK. When I am ready, and it no longer serves me to have it, I will let it go.

For the sake of open disclosure, as I typed this story, I began to sob again. I felt the pain of loss and the consequence of ignoring the pain and stifling the trauma for so many years. I took a moment, allowed myself to grieve for the last time, and now, it appears, I am completely ready to let go of that picture.

Let us not forget that we are powerful beings, but we are also human beings and we should be gentle with ourselves and tend to our needs and honor them, in OUR time.

The exercise of letting go of material attachments enables us not only to take inventory of our needs but also to understand what no longer serves us and to recognize our own personal growth over the years. Additionally, it bleeds into and applies to other aspects of our life on a social and emotional level. These material attachments often keep us from our own emotional development and by releasing them, especially at a young age, we create the foundation for a healthy mindset as we develop throughout our lives. Not to mention, how much easier regular purging makes packing for a move later in life!

Attachment to Belief Systems

We attach ourselves to belief systems as well. These belief systems made us feel safe, secure, and confident in a specific moment of time, but as we grow and develop, we forget to question ourselves about the reason for the attachment and its relevance to our current state of being.

For my entire young adult life, if I'm being completely honest with myself, from the age of about eleven to about forty-nine years old (I am presently fifty years old), I have in one way or another abused or neglected my body for the sake of physical beauty or athletic prowess. Over the years, I have subscribed to countless diets and exercise programs so as to attain and maintain an ideal that in retrospect was clearly out of my reach. I have taught aerobics, practiced kickboxing, and ran extensively. My pattern of abuse and neglect to my body ran deeply into my psyche. I would push the limits until my body would shut down through a variety of different aches and pains and ailments or sheer exhaustion, but I ALWAYS pushed on. The real irony is that when I look back at pictures, regardless of that current state of fitness, I always looked healthy and beautiful, but I never experienced peace, joy, or freedom.

In this situation, my attachments were multitudinous:

- **I was attached to the outcome.**
- **I was attached to the results of my exercise rather than the joy of the activity and the appreciation of my body's willingness and ability to achieve what it set out to do.**

I was RARELY in a state of just pure enjoyment of the activity. I would run every morning for years along the beach while watching the sunrise, a beauty which was often lost on me because I was more focused on my heart rate and self-imposed benchmarks of excellence.

I was attached to my belief systems:

- **No pain, no gain**—if I don't push myself and sacrifice my comfort level, there is nothing to gain in the situation.

- **Anything worth having is worth fighting for**—if I nurture myself and my body, I can't have a body that I love and appreciate.

- **"Go to school, you'll feel better."**—something that I heard my whole childhood, which was a blatant dismissal of any sickness or physical ailment.

- **I believed that if I slowed down just for a moment, I would lose momentum and control of everything I had worked for.**

- **I believed that my self-worth was enmeshed in how I looked. If I didn't look a certain way, I was not worthy of love.**

My attachment to my beliefs was not reviewed, assessed, or put in check for almost forty years! I abused my body for almost four decades because my attachment to my beliefs were so embedded in my psyche. My attachment to my beliefs was what kept me in patterns and paradigms that no longer served me, assuming they ever did. My attachment to my beliefs robbed me of the joy of embracing my body in my favorite outfits or a new swimsuit. It robbed me of the joy of confidently walking down to the water at the beach. It robbed me of the joy of knowing my worthiness to receive love regardless of the number on the scale. It robbed me of the joy of truly loving myself without condition or expectation.

We have to remember that we develop our core beliefs at a very young age, and the patterns that we create based on these beliefs are created by a young, underdeveloped mind. All of the previously mentioned beliefs were developed during adolescence. I was a teenage girl. A teenage girl! At forty years old, I was recreating patterns and paradigms in my life based on the belief system created by a fourteen-year-old teenager! And not only that, if challenged, I vehemently protected that belief system, sometimes just like a fourteen-year-old child would. "No, I will not slow down! Just give me a knee brace. I'll be fine!"

This is one example, but our attachment to our belief systems AND our identities are strong.

Yes, we attach ourselves to our identity; after all, our identities are based on our beliefs about ourselves.

Identifying ourselves as something or someone that can be perceived by others in a complimentary fashion is often comforting to us as well.

I am an athlete: Athletes are strong, attractive, and resilient. I like that. I am an athlete, therefore, I am all of these things. Now I must protect this identity at all costs because if I don't, I am no longer comforted by having this identity.

How many times have you heard yourself or someone else say, "*I'm the type of person that...*" If this declaration of identity is remotely unpalatable, then how many times have you heard yourself or another say, "*I'm this way because...*" Even if the identity is an uncomfortable one, with an excuse for it, it'll still do the trick. Our attachment to our beliefs about the world and ourselves makes us feel safe, but when they cause us more harm than good, they no longer serve us.

At the age of eleven, twelve, thirteen, and fourteen, it was important that I learn the importance of a good work ethic, the importance of maintaining a healthy body and body image, but the messages I received for motivation weren't always received from those with the healthiest perspectives, and at the end of the day, they were received and perceived by an eleven, twelve, thirteen to fourteen-year-old girl.

When we create the habit of regularly checking in with our beliefs about the world and our beliefs about our personal identity, we can ask ourselves:

1. Is this a rational belief based on evidence and a healthy mindset?
2. Does this belief system serve me?
3. Why am I so attached to a way of thinking and being that no longer serves me (if it ever did)?

Then and only then can we make the proper changes in our habits and behaviors. Once we begin to reset and redirect our beliefs without attachment, because as we have more experiences, our beliefs about the world and ourselves will change again...and again...and again, we will be able to once again ignite the joy in our lives.

Attachment to Career Identity

In my thirties, I was single for the majority of that decade. I spent a lot of time in bars and social situations and went on more bad dates than I could count. I have had many varying experiences, but the one thing that remained constant across the board was the first question after

"What's your name?" was ALWAYS "What do you do?"

Prior to my present career as a creative person, I was a career educator for many years. I began my career at twenty-two years old as a special education teacher, specializing in behavioral modification. I then concluded my career as the director of student development in a private high school where I worked for sixteen years, the bulk of my career.

My job began as a learning specialist (where I assisted a small population of students with unique learning styles) and as a classroom teacher. It evolved over the decade with my learning to wear many hats, which included managing all things for exceptional student education and all things related to behavioral modification. Because I was hired during the school's third year, my responsibilities evolved with the evolution of the school, and without listing all of my responsibilities, in essence my primary responsibility felt as if it was to restore order in a sea of chaos.

I was thirty years old when I began working at YHS, and I took a lot of pride in my career path. Remember, my personal life was lacking, and my success in my career was the part of my identity with which I took much pride.

I was a natural educator. My responsibilities spoke to my skill set. I was well respected by both the faculty and students, and much of the frustrating aspects of the job spoke to my irrational beliefs about how *life was hard*. My head of school adored me and gave me carte blanche to be authentic in my approach, which was in many ways unconventional, and he appreciated me for it. I truly took pride in my role as educator and keeper of order.

After having worked there for about a decade or so, three things happened within the span of a few years that shifted my identity.

1. I had children, and my priorities shifted from being a career driven rock star to wanting to be home with my children rather than continue the 'come early, stay late' mentality.

2. Our head of school resigned and was replaced by a man whose philosophy on education was completely contradictory to mine.

3. I began to paint.

I felt the shift but resisted it and continued in a position that for four years gradually became more and more uncomfortable, then unbearable, then impossible to continue.

At the time, I became extremely angry at the changes and the powers that be because the school that I loved so much began to deteriorate, and I was unable to control its new trajectory. At the time, I saw it as black or white, right or wrong, victim or victor. I was so heartbroken by the unhealthy changes in the student population, level of discipline, and standard of education that had occurred in such a short amount of time and how many of these changes had such an adverse effect on my own personal responsibilities at the school. I then spent the last two years there in misery, feeling sick to my stomach, asking, "why am I coming here every day", and pulling out my eyelashes in anger and protest. It was bad, and the toxicity that I brought with me every day was invasive to the other faculty members, and in hindsight, was an embarrassment to me. I had such rancor for "the establishment", that I held hard feelings for an entire year after I resigned.

In retrospect, I learned much about myself and this experience. I learned that for sixteen years, a dozen of which I was a single woman without children, my entire identity was attached to my career, and when my career began to shift, I resisted, causing me extreme discomfort.

When I became a mother during that process, a part of me was conflicted, but the shift of the power structure was something to project my own feelings of inner conflict and confusion about my previous identity as a career driven woman. When I began to paint, my escape from this hell trap became clearer to me, but still I held such anger because my level of attachment to the job was so powerful.

Granted, all of the circumstances that I mentioned were indeed true and created the perfect circumstances for me to move on, but my attachment to my identity, the identity that I held for much of my adult life, is what caused me such extreme discomfort. My fear of letting go and ultimately not knowing who I was outside of my position is what robbed me of my peace.

Presently, I offer the service of intuitive guidance at Ubuntu Fish Gallery. Recently, I have noticed a high concentration of women in their early fifties that are struggling with a similar grieving process and loss of identity. Many of them have followed all the rules—got the right education, the right job, married the right guy, had the great kids, sent them off to the right schools. These women spent the bulk of their adult lives doing the "right thing" by conventional standards, and now their identity as wife and mother has shifted and they have become lost and fearful of who they are or who they are NOT, for that matter.

This is a common occurrence in our culture. Often the first question we ask one another is, "What do you do?"

not, "What do you like?" "What are your creative outlets?" "What makes you happy?" As a result, many of us have forgotten the answers to these questions, leaving us lost and without an identity outside of our work.

I had no idea that my self-worth was so enmeshed with my success as a career educator, and when that career was on the ropes because of several reasons, many of them that were beyond my control, the reality of it all kicked my ass for a while. I wanted to point the finger in every direction but at myself, but what I realize now is nothing is permanent and like everything else, my identity is forever changing, and like everything else, my attachment to any of it is not only futile but robs me of my peace and freedom.

Attachment to Relationships

Our attachment to relationships is what I find most fascinating. My initial premise in the Second Recommandment was that our purpose in this world is for personal growth and expansion and to experience joy and love while doing so. Believing that and believing that our emotional guidance system helps us navigate these experiences so we can learn what brings us joy (often by experiencing what does not bring us joy), it would be safe to assume that this would include ALL of our experiences, including those that we have within and throughout our relationships.

In essence, our relationships gift us opportunities for us to learn about ourselves. Take a second and think about all of the cool stuff we learn from the experiences we have in our relationships. However, if we lose sight of this concept, relationships can become very toxic, and the experiences can become more painful than necessary.

Our most impactful relationships are those of our immediate family—our parents and siblings, then our extended family—aunts, uncles, grandparents, cousins, and close family friends. These relationships offer us the most opportunity for growth and expansion and set the foundation for future relationships by setting the stage for our beliefs about ourselves and the world at large. This is why the emotions are so intense with these "teachers", because the lessons are the most extreme and important in many cases. Remember, our emotions are here to lead us from what we don't want and guide us to what we do want for ourselves. Forgetting this hinders us from fully integrating the experience and keeps us stuck, attaching the emotion to the experience and never quite processing the experience in its entirety. THIS is how irrational beliefs are born! THIS is where the unhealthy patterns begin!

Once our foundation is in place and we begin to develop outside of our immediate family, we integrate school teachers, school age peers, and friends into our lives as lesson bearers. This rotation of lesson bearers continues throughout our lives—colleagues, interpersonal relationships, spouses, eventually our own children, and so on.

The more intimate the relationship, the more powerful the lessons, and the more intense the emotions attached to them.

It all makes sense! What could possibly go wrong? Well, this:

1. As mentioned in the Second Recommandment, *I Shalt Not Become Entrenched in My Emotions*, because the emotions in our formative years are so intense and because our caretakers aren't always armed with this insight, the lessons often become muddied, unlearned, and the child is often left learning an unhealthy belief system about themselves or the world in which they live.

2. Because somewhere along the line, we have been conditioned to believe that there must be a loyalty to our relationships based on longevity and genetic

connection, we often remain in relationships that no longer serve us, and we continue to live and experience discontentment.

If we believe that it's in our highest good to let go of experiences, habits, relationships, and beliefs that no longer serve us, and if we believe that the people in our lives are there so we can learn, grow, and evolve, then why do we remain in relationships that contradict both statements?

It would be equivalent to continuing to wear the same size seven shoe from middle school because we've known each other for the last forty years! I grew out of size seven by the time I entered high school, and with each stage in life, I found myself in a size ten. Then I had children, and now I sport an eleven. I didn't even know they made that size shoe, but I digress.

The point is, I hold no attachment to something that once served me but no longer does so now, even if we have longevity in our relationship. I appreciate all the times we have spent together. I appreciate all the places these shoes have taken me. There is no ill will; I just no longer fit in those shoes, nor do I resonate with that style, and that's OK.

With that said, it is not always necessary to forge personal sovereignty, burn bridges, or declare official breakups. Sometimes a clean break is important and necessary, but sometimes a restructuring of the current relationship is what will do the trick. Sometimes, just having awareness of the purpose of these relationships is all that you need to take the sting out of the discomfort that the lessons in these relationships offer.

Your discernment is important here. Removing yourself from being entrenched in the emotional aspect of the relationship will help you gain objectivity, and with that objectivity, you will have more clarity on how (if at all) that relationship serves you.

Resonance and Dissonance

Most relationships begin with a certain resonance, an energetic connection or vibration—a chemistry, if you will. When you meet someone new, there are often immediate signs of resonance. When you resonate with other people's energy, it feels good. You may have many things in common, or you may just enjoy being in their company. Either way, this resonance lures you into the beginnings of a relationship. At that moment in time, it may not be clear, but you each have something to offer the other in terms of personal growth and development.

Early in the relationship, there are usually more experiences that help you understand what you want.

Ohhh, I like this, so I want more of this.

As the relationship progresses, the dreaded red flags appear, and our emotions signal us to those flags.

Oh, I don't much care for that.

But rather than see the emotional signal for what it is, we often ignore it because we want more of the *good feelings* to happen or we ignore the *not so good feelings* because our attachment to the expectation of the outcome of the relationship is stronger than the signal to the lesson.

What happens next? Well, the signals become louder, the emotional response becomes more intense, and we often become so entrenched in those emotions that we lose sight of the purpose of the emotional signal. We begin to feel victimized by the other's "unacceptable" behavior, and we often revert to our patterns of coping that were created in childhood that likely no longer serve us, thus creating the same pattern that were experienced many times before. Next thing we know, we are finding ourselves in yet another unpleasant relationship that ultimately will end with bad feelings and very little learned.

- What if we tried something different?
- What if we recognized the first "icky" feelings and treated them like a warning shot?
- What if we tried remaining in the relationship but with the understanding that there is something to learn about ourselves here?
- What if we observed the situation with more objectivity and clarity and responded to that warning shot with a healthy, adult driven response?

By doing this, the purpose of personal growth and expansion is being met, and as a result of this new way of being, two possibilities emerge:

1. You learn and grow, and your partner has an opportunity to also learn and grow through this healthy shared experience.
2. You learn and grow, and your partner does not take this opportunity to learn and grow with you. This is when you begin to feel some dissonance, and the ickiness gets ickier.

When you recognize that your joyful personal evolution is the key to your own empowerment, happiness, and well-being, you will begin to engage the process of conflict with a whole new perspective.

If your partner witnesses your approach, they may adopt it or act in fear of it and revert to their comfortable approach that no longer serves you or the relationship. Gradually, the dissonance between you and your partner becomes terribly uncomfortable for the both of you. *For clarity, partner does not necessarily mean romantic partner; any person with whom you are engaging in a relationship, from a friend or coworker to your neighbor, can be considered a partner for the sake of my point.*

Now what?

It appears to me that you have four options:

1. You can recognize that if your partner's resolution of a conflict is not resonant with your own, you may attempt to teach or show them another way, but unfortunately this approach is often met with resistance, because as mentioned in previous text, we protect our beliefs, behaviors, and patterns vehemently.

2. You can continue the relationship, remaining steadfast in your approach to conflict resolution, but if your partner continues to reject growing,

learning, and resonating with you, the relationship will continue to cause you discomfort.

3. You can restructure the relationship by creating boundaries that are in alignment with what best serves you, i.e. "Maybe we'd be better as friends."

4. You can recognize that you've learned all there is to learn from this relationship, and the discomfort now outweighs the benefits, and it's time to create distance or move on completely.

Because of our attachment to relationships, it becomes difficult to perceive them in a logical manner, but when we balance our emotional side with our logical side, it becomes easier to navigate these uncomfortable experiences in a healthier manner.

The Pitfalls of Continuing Dissonant Relationships

From what I've learned about the nature of relationships over the years, I have become pretty adept at recognizing the dissonance relatively early on, and as a result, extracting the lesson and ultimately exiting the relationship.

The degrees of my exits have ranged from Atom bomb, to full-on blowtorch, to sledgehammer, to just quietly pulling back my energy and allowing nature to take its course. Obviously, the more adept I become at this skill, the less likely I am to leave collateral damage in my wake.

Yes, it does get yucky sometimes, but the stinkiest pile of doo doo often creates the most fertile ground for our personal growth. Remember, these are emotions. Some relationships are more intimate than others, making this process extremely difficult at times, and in general terms, this is hard, and we are ALL learning.

With awareness and practice, the lessons and the transition out of these relationships become much easier, and you will begin to understand how remaining in these relationships under the guise of "love" or "loyalty" or "obligation" or a "need of some sort" is detrimental to your own personal growth.

My Mother's Death Bed

My mother's passing was probably one of the most profoundly difficult opportunities for personal growth that I have ever had. As I had mentioned in the prologue, my relationship with my mother had always been tenuous at best, and in the last few years of her life, it grossly deter-iorated into a bitter estrangement, lasting until she was literally on her death bed.

Regardless of the toxicity of our relationships, when these relationships are of the greatest intimacy, such as lovers, parents, children, and siblings, the waters of loyalty become quite muddied. The attachment to these relationships is built on hardwired beliefs and condition-ing that are woven so deeply into our patterns and paradigms.

"What do you mean...but he's your brother!"

"That's not right...that's your mother!"

"You can't do that... he's the father of your child!"

Because of the nature of my backstory, my ability to see past these familial obligations is a little more in tune than most, and I seem to be a little more at ease cutting these seemingly uncuttable detachments. I have had family members turn their backs on me at the drop of a dime and re-enter my life with the same rapidity. Because I spent most of my adult life as "an island", I have learned to free myself, to some degree, from obligatory attachments with little guilt or shame.

My mother, however, was the more challenging rela-tionship from which to detach, not because of the level of intimacy, but rather because of my conditioned beliefs of disrespect and disloyalty for doing so. When my mother declared war just prior to my wedding, I understood on a much deeper level that I had only two choices:

1. Continue to engage in a relationship paradigm that fed unhealthy beliefs about myself and ALWAYS left me feeling shitty.
2. End the relationship because there was absolutely no evidence of a healthy reconciliation that was based on reconstructed boundaries of love, trust, and respect.

During the first year after my wedding, there were still missiles fired from my mother's camp, validating my understanding and concretizing my decision to choose the latter. I never responded to the missiles, and regardless of how unpopular that decision was among my mother's loving friends, I understood that this decision was best for me. My husband, who had been my rock as I put myself back together piece by piece, completely supported me in my decision.

For the next three years after the wedding, my life blossomed into something truly miraculous. My children were happy, healthy, and thriving. My relationship with my father was evolving into something I could never have imagined, and through that relationship, I had reconciled with much of my paternal family that for my entire adult life were only childhood memories for me. My husband was (and is) the Schmoopiest of all Schmoopies and was now the girls' legal father, having adopted them in 2015. I began to paint, continued to paint, and was preparing to leave my career in education in June 2017 to pursue a career as an artist. I was seeing myself through the eyes of my husband and my girls and learning to love myself like I had never done before. By the summer of 2017, I was thriving in a way that I never thought possible, and then I got the text from my brother who had so much venom for me that I actually felt my stomach turn when I received the notification.

The text read: *Your mother is full of cancer. You might want to come visit her before she dies.*

If my memory serves, I'm pretty sure he threw in a jab about how I kept her grandchildren from her too. So, now what? As far as I could see it, after the shock of my brother's word choice wore off, once again, I had two choices:

1. I could succumb to the pressure of my mother/ daughter bond, my family attachment, or my desire

to see my mother one last time, but the truth is I felt none of that. The truth is I had grieved the loss of my mother and said goodbye so many times before, and I had said goodbye for the last time in an extremely painful way three years prior.

2. I could succumb to the pressure of my conditioned response to the attachment, *worrying about what would people say?* and muscle up and *do the right thing*, which would place me right in the center of a hornets' nest, a place I had no interest in residing.

Weddings and funerals are a funny thing; they bring out such intensity of emotion in people. You truly get to see who people are under these circumstances, and I had already seen the first act; I was not sticking around for Act II.

Once I cleared myself of many of my irrational beliefs from childhood and learned my worthiness and how to treat myself with care, love, and respect, I became able to make the difficult decisions with much more clarity and more resolve. I began to trust my inner guidance system and allow myself to make decisions based on love, love for

MYSELF, rather than guilt and fear about how I'd be perceived. Not only did I know immediately that I would not go, but I also knew that my brother's text did not require a response.

Over my years of actively reversing the momentum of my own traumatic experiences, I witnessed something very interesting in the formula of doing the work. This is not by any means a scientific discovery, but it is something I have observed repeatedly along the way. Once we decide and begin making moves to shift our trajectories, we are presented with an opportunity to renege on our decision. When I surprisingly got pregnant at thirty-seven years old by a man with whom I saw no future and having had no real desire to have children of my own, while also working in a religious institution, which would drastically jeopardize my job and shift my trajectory, I had to carefully consider what I wanted to do. I decided that yes, regardless of the circumstances, I wanted to have a child. Four weeks later, I miscarried. *How bad do you want it, Dana?* Well, I wanted it badly enough that I intentionally became pregnant with my first-born daughter two months later.

Shortly after I made the decision to leave a well-paying, stable job to pursue my passion for painting, which involved selling our house, moving to a rural area, and giving up the fancy car amongst other luxuries, I was then offered a similar job to the one I was leaving, making $175,000 a year. *How bad do you want it, Dana?* Well, I wanted it badly enough that I gave up both jobs, the house by the beach, and the Mercedes, so I could paint in the woods until I figured it out.

When you make a decision that is life-changing and for your highest good, these opportunities will arise. *How badly do you want it, your name here?* **That's for YOU to decide. THAT'S the work!**

When I was faced with that question once again after trudging knee deep through a shit swamp for the decade prior, the answer was a no brainer. Regardless of the perceived attachments or the perceived obligations, the answer to the question *How badly do I want my self-worth, my self-love, and my self-respect?* Oh, I want it. I want it bad!

Two months later, I received a message from a distant family friend on Facebook, wishing me her condolences. That's the day that I learned of my mother's passing. After the initial punch to the gut, I felt no regret and never looked back.

It's important to note that although I relate this story

with conviction, it is an uncomfortable story to tell, but it's also important to note that I am neither bitter nor cold-hearted; I just finally and truly gave myself permission to be happy and to ask myself not just, *What does Dana want?* but also *What does Dana need?* and to have the courage and empowerment and worthiness to get it.

My observation of my own personal relationships has revealed the following to me:

1. Regardless of the nature of the relationship and my belief about the loyalty to the relationship, if the relationship is toxic to my well-being and beginning to hinder my growth rather than serve it, it is time to either alter, distance myself, or exit the relationship.

2. When I move on from a relationship, I have ALWAYS learned something from it, even if it is as simple as *I'll never do that again!*

3. I attract people who are in alignment with who I am and what I need in that moment of time.

4. These relationships are here to help me work through my own imbalances and irrational beliefs, patterns, and paradigms that I've picked up along the way.

5. All relationships have an impact, not just the

familial and romantic relationships.

6. My next relationship always reflects or showcases this new aspect of myself that was revealed in my last relationship.

7. By staying in an uncomfortable relationship longer than necessary, because I thought I could change things by force, love, or persuasion, I had been doing myself a disservice.

8. The more adept I become at discerning the emotional signals, objectively perceiving the situation, learning the lessons, and cycling through the relationship when it no longer serves me, the quicker I develop as a human being, thus attracting even more like-minded people with whom to create more relationships.

9. The more I do this, the easier it gets, and the easier it gets the more magical and self-aware people come into my life, AND the more magical and self-aware the people are, the more likely they are to resonate with my way of being and choose to grow and develop with me rather than without me.

10. The process becomes easier when I ask myself, *Does this serve me?* in these experiences and when I honor the answer.

Attachment to Outcome

For me, attachment to outcome has been my most difficult challenge to overcome, and if I am not paying attention, I can easily slip back into this habit. Attachment to outcome truly robs us of our joy.

When I was working as an educator, by happenstance, I picked up a paintbrush for the first time since childhood and began a journey of self-discovery that I could not even have imagined. Painting that first painting was exhilarating! It felt so good to paint. At the time, my children were young, four and five years old. I would come home from work every evening, feed them, spend time with them, put them to bed, and then put a sheet on the dining room table and paint until my neck and shoulders would no longer allow me to paint.

At the time, I could never have guessed that this joyful endeavor would eventually lead me to leaving my job, selling my house, moving out to the country, creating my own merchandise, opening a gallery, writing books; the list goes on. All I knew in those moments when I painted was the joy inside of me was beyond measure. The body of work that I created in the first few years was beyond anybody's comprehension, and it was solely because it brought me joy.

What I noticed, however, was that when I was commissioned to do a painting, the process became more stressful because what was once me doing what felt good to me, became trying to achieve an ideal (for someone else) and having an attachment to the outcome. This attachment robbed me of my joy to a degree.

As my painting progressed, being able to find success as an artist began to become clear to me. I began to create the story of my success in my head and focus on the steps to get there. I was so focused and aggressive in my pursuits, and as a result, I really made some strides towards what I perceived as success at the time.

I began painting in 2015. By 2016, I had my first exhibition, and I had sold several pieces. By 2017, I was doing art festivals, had two more exhibitions, and quit my job. By 2018, I had a few more exhibitions, a website, was featured in a magazine, and made the newspaper. The whole experience continued to bring me joy because even though I had a desire for success, my attachment to it was minimal, and I was truly enjoying EVERYTHING the artist experience had to offer.

In 2019, I opened Ubuntu Fish Gallery in Stuart, Florida. Still, this was beyond anything I could have imagined and still some of the most exciting and joyful days of my life. Once the doors were open and the dust had settled, I noticed something different about my painting. Although I truly enjoyed painting, there was a level of pressure when I decided to paint a new piece, and sometimes I would get stuck without inspiration. There was a level of expectation and attachment to the outcome that did not exist in the early days. It is like comparing how a fifteen-year-old teenager and a five-year-old child would approach playing soccer. One with a direct intention—to win—and the other playing for the joy of the game. One child intense and focused and the other laughing, playing, and kicking a ball around. Like the fifteen-year-old teenager, I noticed my spark for the joy of painting diminished a bit during the process of achieving.

Presently, I am well into the process of balancing being and doing, and retrospection has helped me return to the pleasures of now. I'm now allowing the chips to fall where they may and truly enjoying the experience for the experience, and this new perspective has changed my life.

And I'll tell you some secret special insights that I picked up through this experience.

Society has trained us to be achievement-oriented. Attain, attain, achieve, achieve, attain some more, but it never stops. I learned that my "to-do" list will never be completed, so THEN I can relax. My "to-do" list will always have something to do on it. ALWAYS.

I also learned that it is human nature to desire more than what we are or what we have. It is an inherent part of our genetic make-up, and that's ok and necessary for our personal growth—BUT it is because of our attachment to these desires that we suffer.

In Buddhist philosophy of The Four Noble Truths, the first three read as follows:

- Everything in life is suffering.

- We suffer because of our attachments or desires.

- To end the suffering, we must end these attachments or desires.

Although I agree with these statements, I believe if misconstrued, it could potentially exacerbate people's suffering. To end desire is contradictory to the human make-up and the human experience. Experiencing love, joy, and expansion comes with desire. Desire is necessary in order to know what you want.

The key is nonattachment.

I personally want to be a successful creative person—author, artist, illustrator, intuitive—but that success is releasing the attachment to the outcome. You see, my success is not only measured by the joy I feel in the moments that I am doing what I love, but also the probabilities of my success could manifest in a variety of ways.

If I attach myself to a specific outcome—it becomes a pass or fail exam. It becomes only right or wrong. My attachment to the outcome considerably decreases my chances of any outcome that serves me AND robs me of my joy of the experience.

If I continue to do what I love and feel the joy in what I'm doing and involve myself in behaviors and patterns that only serve me, then my outer world has no choice but to reflect and project my emotions, beliefs, and actions.

It's all starting to make sense now, isn't it? You steer this ship. YOU. Only you, and when you realize this, life becomes magical.

Trust me. You're reading my book, right 😊.

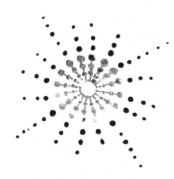

Seventh

Recommandment

I shalt not refute the truth and deny the solution to that truth.

Rather, I shall accept that awareness and willingness are the keys to wellness. If I am not well, then I may lack the awareness or the understanding of the problem at hand or the solution to that problem. If I have the awareness, and am still not well, then I am lacking the willingness to do what is necessary to rectify the problem at hand.

Acceptance of these truths is the first step in the right direction. I also understand that anger, frustration, and discontent are just a form of resistance to the truth, and my readiness to accept this truth is my first step toward freedom.

In the Sixth Recommandment, I had discussed in detail the variety of ways we create attachments and the level in which we protect them. Many of us understand the *why* for the way we are and the *where* from which our way of being originated. We accept that *because this happened to me, I now behave in this way*, and this becomes our truth. Then we become attached to our truth, and speak our truth, and revel in our truth, and feel victimized by our truth, and desire a different truth but then defend our truth because, well, it's our truth!

We despise our truths, yet we embrace them, and even in some cases, wear them as a badge of honor, because accepting the truth of *how I turned out like this* is somehow more palatable when we know someone else is responsible for it.

Ironically, we often find it more comfortable to live in our stories and to live with the consequences of this unhappy truth than to actually face the truth in its entirety, which is *because this happened to me, I behave this way, but because I am a sovereign being who writes my own script, I have the power to change my truth through shifting my beliefs and altering my patterns whenever I so choose.*

The awareness of our truth is crucial to our wellness, but the awareness alone is like diagnosing an illness and then calling it a day! The diagnosis is Step 1. What about Steps, 2, 3, and 4 and so on? Often, we get stuck in Step 1 because our feelings of shame and hopelessness cloud our ability to see any other way of being, but with a little clarity and the willingness to shift this belief system step by step, we can unstick ourselves and become empowered.

EXAMPLE:

I cannot maintain a healthy relationship.

Step 1: Identify the causality of my inability to maintain a relationship.

Because my mother was emotionally distant and I felt abused and abandoned by my father, I never truly knew how to properly love another. That's why I can't maintain a relationship!

Step 2: Identify my beliefs that are a result of this childhood programming.

I am only worthy of relationships that are abusive or neglectful.

Step 3: Identify the patterns that I have created in my life based on this belief about myself.

Actually, I do choose partners that either abuse me or neglect me in different ways.

Come to think of it, this is how I treat myself quite often.

I also tend to overcompensate in relationships so as to receive the love that I am not receiving from others.

Now that I am looking at this more clearly, I sometimes sabotage relationships, so I don't get disappointed by them as I have in all my previous relationships.

If I'm being completely honest with myself, I tend to self-protect with anger and sometimes create distance, so that I don't get hurt again, and when you think about it, I suppose my behavior can be perceived by another as abusive and neglectful...hmmm...

Hey, it's uncomfortable to be this honest with myself! I don't want to do this anymore. Maybe I should have a drink or eat a cookie or take a selfie or buy something I don't need so I can feel better.

Hey, wait, isn't distracting myself and ultimately placing blame on the cause part of the problem, and truly the only way I am going to rectify this problem once and for all is by my awareness of it in its entirety and my willingness to do the work by looking at it, taking responsibility for addressing it, and sticking with it even know it's hard?

Hmmmm, there is something to this nonsense. I think I have learned something here...grrrrr.

OK, OK, OK, I've gone completely off the rails with this example, but I think you get my point. Looking at ourselves is difficult, and attaining this level of self-awareness is difficult, but having the willingness to do so is just so rewarding.

I get that there is such a level of fear attached to looking at ourselves under a microscope. Many of us are our own worst critics and already carry so much guilt, shame, and fear that has been assigned to us by others over the years because others, unfortunately, did not have the tools to rectify their own guilt, shame, and fear, so they've projected it onto us in a myriad of unique and creative ways. Whether they gifted us their fear through shared experiences or thoughtless words or just their own lack of awareness, they've passed it to us as it was passed onto them. Fear is truly the gift that keeps on giving, and when we know better we will do better, with awareness and willingness.

We've looked at it. We've examined it. We've seen Grandma naked, and there is no unseeing it. Now what?

Phase 2: Willingness

How do we undo all the naked Grandma stuff? How do we get some clothes on this woman!?

Frankly, I don't have the answer to these questions because the answer is different for all of us. I often joke with clients when they share a tragic story which has created an unhealthy belief system. I kiddingly jab at them, "You know, you're not special, right?" I am half teasing, but what I am trying to convey is that we are ALL going through the same thing. The players have different faces and names, and the details are different, but we are ALL working to find our own peace and freedom. The principles are universal, but the execution varies with each of us.

This is such an important concept to remember because during these challenging times, and with the uncertainty of our own decision-making process, we begin to look outward for guidance, which is often helpful, but at the end of the day, what works for another may not be the right fit for you. Receiving advice and guidance is a beautiful thing and essential for a broader perspective but asking yourself, "What is one step I can take in this moment to move closer to contentment?" is fool proof and the first step to getting Grandma covered up!

Having an awareness of the root cause and of your behavioral patterns is half the battle; the other half resides in your willingness to make the difficult decisions and take the necessary steps for what's in your best interest. It is easy to fall back on distractions and old habits for self-soothing. It feels comfortable to rely on gurus that have all the answers. It feels safe to rely on rituals and practices and allow them to do the work for you, but by following some of the techniques presented in the previous recommend-ments, and with continued commitment to yourself and your well-being, Grandma will be dressed in no time.

Eighth Recommandment

I shalt not abuse my body with words, substances, food, actions or neglect it by ignoring its messages when it speaks to me.

Rather, I SHALL embrace my body, treat it with love and respect, trust my physical guidance system, and rely on any information that it offers, telling me that something in my physical vessel is in need of attention.

In Ancient Egypt, after a person died, Egyptians performed a ritual of weighing their heart in order to grant access to the afterlife. The belief was that the lighter the heart, the more good deeds a person had done in their lifetime, and therefore, they could be permitted to enter the afterlife. A heavy heart would restrict such access.

In modern times, we use expressions such as *with a heavy heart* to express sadness or regret or *light-hearted* to express being carefree and happy. This concept of our emotional state affecting our physicality is an ancient concept that has been with the human race for millennia. Not only do I believe that there is something very valid to the idea of the heart carrying the weight of our emotions, but I also believe this concept goes way beyond the heart.

As all human beings have an emotional guidance system, they too have a physical guidance system. The physical body is an extremely intelligent, informational network that assists us in detecting fear, joy, pain, and overall dysfunction within our being. It works in concert with the emotional guidance system, and when we properly tune into the signals and messages it sends us, we can not only navigate life with more ease, but we can also detect misalignments within ourselves much more readily and without experiencing extreme physical consequences and maladies.

There are many resources available that support this theory. I highly recommend the documentary *Heal*, which appears on Gaia and the book *You Can Heal Your Life*, by Louise Hay, but for the sake of my point, I will rely on logic, common sense, and my own personal experience.

The ways in which our emotions and physical responses work together to reveal to us our general state of being is so precise, but often we are either too entrenched in our emotions to receive the messages or too busy and distracted to receive the physical signals. We are guided by the belief that a prescription or external remedy is a better option, or we are just in complete denial that any of this is even a thing to consider for our wellness.

Today, I will offer an example of *entrenchment in emotions* that is actually happening in real time so we can unravel it together.

This morning, I lost my temper with my daughter's bus driver. Not my finest moment, but here is what happened. Nadia's scheduled pick-up time is 6:41am at the front of our complex approximately half a mile from my home. Yes, I know it's super early for a 4th grader to be at the bus stop, but let's do our best to hold judgement during this story.

Presently, Nadia is the only child at this bus stop, so my husband and I alternate transporting her there because it's dark and it's far. Because the development where we live is new and the bus stop is new, there have been glitches and inconsistencies with bus arrival from the word *go*. Early on in the school year, the bus began arriving at approximately 6:30am because another bus stop was added to the route. Fortunately, my husband is chronically early, so he would take Nadia to the bus stop super early anyway, and the transition was relatively seamless. Throughout the year, there have been several cases when there has been a substitute bus driver, who had been observing the original bus route 6:41am and had even run late according to that schedule, and at times has not even shown up. The inconsistencies to some degree were becoming more like consistencies.

Recently, Rob's work schedule had changed, and I

began dropping Nadia off at the bus stop more regularly. During this time, I had noticed there had been several instances when the bus arrived at 6:45am, 6:50am, and one day the bus hadn't come at all. I had a conversation with the bus driver about the inconsistent arrival times, and he told me he would be there without fail between 6:28am and 6:31am, and although I was never happy with this time, I accepted this information.

This morning, I was not as punctual as usual, and I sped Nadia to the bus stop and pulled up as my clock turned 6:28am, and the bus was just pulling away. I'm not sure he even stopped. I pulled up next to him, inciting him to pull over. I was furious and said some things. Yeah, I said things.

Here is where the heart heaviness begins:

I immediately regretted speaking with him in that way. I felt embarrassed and ashamed and couldn't shed the feeling that I just dropped the F bomb to the bus driver with my kid in earshot. As much as I have the tools to work through these situations, I began to ruminate about the situation. I caught myself justifying my behavior, internally citing examples of how he had it coming because of blah, blah, and blah. Having a modicum of self-awareness, I did my best to put that unhealthy coping skill to rest.

I then began to excuse my behavior with the *I really didn't sleep well* and the *I'm feeling hormonal* self-talk. Both true statements, but I put that to rest also. When I returned home, I cried a little bit because I felt so dumb. Then, I just sat in quiet until I got some clarity on what to do, because regardless of the details of the circumstance, I behaved the way I did because A. I'm a human being, B. I was feeling vulnerable physically, and C. I felt powerless over the situation.

Then it came to me. My frustration had been brewing from the day school began when I had faced extreme resistance and frustration while trying to get both of my children assigned buses and stops. It was truly complicated and anxiety inducing from day one. Secondly, there had been many inconsistencies throughout the school year with the bus's arrival, and I never trusted that it would show up, stirring up anxiety every morning that I ignored. Lastly, I was feeling vulnerable because physically I wasn't feeling well, and I overreacted to what I had been able to ignore previously. So, I ruminated on what happened, which exacerbated my feelings of embarrassment and anger and disempowerment for a bit before I figured out *What can I do in this moment to get one step closer to feeling contentment?*

Then, I called the bus company and left a voicemail for Randy with whom I had a relationship from our previous "Where's the bus?" conversations. I apologetically explained that I had words with the bus driver. Then, I asked that he call me to discuss next year's bus schedule so we could be prepared for what's to come and we could suss out any inconsistencies so as to streamline the process for all involved.

When I hung up, minus the uncomfortable feeling of knowing I had to apologize to the bus driver the following morning, I felt better, lighter, and relieved because I had taken action. It was a minor action, but it was what I was able to do in that moment to feel better, and I did it.

I wanted to call my husband and bitch about how wronged I was by the Martin County Department of Transportation, and I wanted to eat a cupcake with my coffee because it would make me feel better, but I didn't, and my heart has lightened up.

I share this story of the minutiae of my life because these are stories that we as human beings face on a moment-to-moment basis all day, every single day of our lives. I have faced millions of similar stories in the past and many, many, MANY previous versions of myself had handled them completely differently. I would like to think that in a few of them I might not have cursed at the bus driver, but either way, the follow ups to the "incident" would all look the same.

I would continue to feel shame for my behavior. I would excuse it, then project anger at the other party involved in order to justify my argument that that person had it coming. Then, I would carry those emotions for a while, eventually stuffing them away, feeling on some level burdened by the whole experience.

We all have done this. If you say you haven't, you are lying to yourself, so go back to the Seventh Recommandment, and I'll hold your spot until you're ready for what's next.

In the span of our lives, we have had countless experiences, from those as minor as this one to those so egregious in nature that they cause severe trauma to our emotional and physical vessels. Some have been forgotten, some have been ignored, some have been addressed, but ALL, on some level, remain in our tissues.

I am not a scientist, and this is a difficult concept to explain, but look at it like wear and tear on a vehicle. If I drive my car heavy on the brakes, my brakes are likely to show signs of damage sooner than in a car that has not had this experience. If I regularly experience unresolved emotional heaviness and continue to compound it with more emotional heaviness, the wear and tear on my physicality will likely manifest into physical maladies at some point.

Everything we do is recorded in our vessel. When we go back and reverse the momentum of our unhealthy beliefs and behaviors, we heal our emotional AND physical bodies, oftentimes releasing the trapped emotions in tears, headaches, unexplainable pains, and more.

Returning to our initial trauma and reversing the damage of the trapped emotions is challenging but very much possible. Our ultimate goal, however, is to cycle through our experiences in a healthy manner in real time, so the tissue doesn't initially hold the heaviness of the emotion, and we can utilize our emotional and physical guidance systems in concert as originally intended.

So today, I cycled through my emotional response in real time, ultimately releasing the anger, guilt, and shame before it got stuck in my physicality. However, what happens to all of the anger, guilt, and shame from previous experiences? It gets stuck.

As a child, when I fell ill or sustained a minor injury, the adults that cared for me often neglected my needs and allowed me to muscle through whatever I was experiencing. The running joke in my house was, "Oh, you're bleeding out the eyes? Go to school; you'll feel better."

The child brain's messages were:

A. *Your health and safety needs are not important.*

B. *Regardless of what your body is telling you, you must trudge forward.*

C. *You are unloved by your caretakers.*

On the flipside, some of us have learned through childhood that the attention and care we may be lacking can be brought to us through sickness and physical dysfunction. Depending on the severity of the childhood experience, this behavior can create the opposite belief system:

A. *When I am sick, I matter.*

B. *I receive love and attention when I am sick.*

C. *When I am not feeling well, EVERYTHING stops.*

As a result of those beliefs, often without realizing, the line of thinking becomes, when I'm sick, my needs matter, and with every symptom, I over address it so as to bring more attention to it and to myself, potentially making myself sicker. I am not suggesting that we intentionally make ourselves sick for attention, but as I've explained repeatedly, the belief of the child gone unchecked creates powerful and unhealthy patterns and paradigms.

By this point, I have beaten beliefs and patterns to death, but humor me here for a second. At a young age, tending to my physical guidance system was stunted, resulting in a pattern of behavior that was not conducive for the best health and wellness decisions in my life. My pattern was to ignore my physical warning signs until they became more severe maladies, which required more serious medical attention. I never even thought to take the time and ask, "What is my body telling me?" or "What emotions am I still carrying from a previous uncomfortable experience?"

Think about it. You have a stressful day; you get a headache. You are worried about something; you get heartburn. Those are obvious manifestations of trapped emotions, but the consequences become more severe and more complicated the more we ignore these minor warning shots. As we age, the more momentum we allow to pick up throughout our lives. We also live in a *seek outwardly for remedies* culture, resulting in us popping pills to solve our aches, pains, and discomforts, but in reality, these *remedies* only confound and compound the issue.

What if we began to look at our ailments a little differently? What if we began to utilize our physical and emotional guidance systems in concert? What if, rather than chugging the Mylanta today, we identify the cause of our stomach woes, reverse engineer the whole thing, and remove the catalyst for the discomfort all together?

New Jersey

When I was 28 years old, I moved back to NJ for two winters before remembering why I originally left in the first place, allowing me to then return to Florida. During that time, I developed terrible stomach problems, resulting in two trips to the Emergency Room. I agreed to an endoscopy, so I could understand the nature of the problem. I was diagnosed with acid reflux, causing Barrett's Esophagitis and prescribed a bland diet and Aciphex to reduce the acid that was causing and exacerbating the diagnosis. Not knowing any better, I endured the tests, accepted the diagnosis, and took the medication.

What I didn't do was take the time to consider the root cause for the pain in my abdomen that was also affecting my esophagus. The emotional factors that created my physical symptoms were as follows: At twenty-eight years old, I returned to NJ after having attended college and after having begun the first few years of my professional career in Florida for the decade prior. I was extremely happy in Florida, but my current teaching job hit a dead end, my roommate and dearest friend with whom I had moved to a new city to live, got a job offer out of state, and my boyfriend at the time had to suddenly move to NY for personal reasons. The first domino of abandonment was toppled. Because I was finding myself lost and without options and thought I was getting to an age that I should probably consider settling down nearer to my family, I landed back in NJ. In essence, my decision was not made from a loving place or for what I thought was in my best interest; rather, it was made in fear and desperation. My decision was not what felt good in my heart and soul, and my body was telling me this, and I was actively ignoring it.

During my time in NJ, I was involved in a tumultuous relationship with my boyfriend. We had a pretty severe fight that resulted in a breakup on the day I moved. Allow me to repeat, on the day I packed up ten years of my life and moved to the place from which I fled a decade prior, my primary reason for moving ended the relationship under extremely painful circumstances that were comp-letely out of my control. Down goes the second domino. I had spent the next two years "working it out" with him so that we could have a failed marriage a few years later. Yes, I am also shaking my head. I was also reacquainted with my maternal family after being on my own for that decade, only to be reminded of why I left and chose to live on my own for the last ten years. I attempted to reacquaint myself with my high school social circles, but everyone had their own lives by this point, and I was no longer the same person. I truly fit in nowhere at this point, and once again turned to food and other substances for comfort—surrounded by a sea of toppled dominos.

It was an extremely dark point in my life. My body not only responded with weight gain, but it also responded by sending signals of dysfunction in the areas of my solar plexus and my throat chakra, showcasing my disem-powerment, my fear of abandonment, my struggle for purpose and personal identity, and my lack of living a life of authenticity.

Unbeknownst to me, my body was screaming at me, and it was doing so loudly. At the time, I did not under-stand the cause of my physical suffering, and if I did, I was trained to ignore it. I knew I was unhappy, but sometimes the momentum of our unhappiness is so strong and exists for so long that we don't even consider making the connection to our experiences or circumstances, or we forget that we even have the ability to change our circumstances and shift them. Instead, we acquiesce and take the pills. I did the latter. Fortunately, however, the winters were harsh. I was cold, so I returned home.

After the second winter, I made the decision to move back to Florida, and that June, almost two years to the day that I left, I was back home. What I came to realize shortly after my return was that I began to feel better in a place that brought me more peace and contentment, and within a few months, I stopped taking the pills, and I never had stomach issues of that severity again.

When I trace back my more serious physical afflictions over the years, I discover two main causes:

1. My pattern of abuse and neglect and its adverse effects on my body.
2. Each affliction directly correlated with a momentum of unresolved emotional trauma.

When I was twenty-five years old, I was diagnosed with thyroid cancer—throat chakra. For most of my twenties and thirties, I had suffered with Bartholin's cysts, endometriosis, and fibroid tumors—sacral chakra. As I previously mentioned, in my late twenties, I experienced acid reflux that created Barrett's Esophagitis—Solar plexus and throat chakras. When I was forty-three years old, I was diagnosed with Rheumatoid Arthritis that in retrospect, I had been symptomatic for at least five years prior—total abuse of my body and neglectful of its signs.

All of these afflictions were treated through traditional medical practices and resulted in procedures, operations, and a variety of medications throughout the years. As for the more ongoing issues, such as the recurring fibroids and Bartholin issues, I have not had an issue since my last surgery in 2015, the year I began painting and embarked on a new journey of self-healing, self-discovery, and self-awareness.

I've learned that thoughts and emotions are a form of energy. E-motions are just energy in motion, and if we look at it logically, if the motion of this energy becomes stagnant or stuck, it creates feelings of heaviness and discomfort that adversely affect our wellness. In order to move that energy, we must first process the emotions that occurred during the traumatic event that elicited them in the first place. Remember, these emotions are meant to guide us, not to hinder our health and wellness. When we allow these emotions to guide us, and we are able to resolve the issues through our actions, the energy moves, alleviating us from having a physical response as a result of the stagnant energy. If the momentum of stored stagnant energy builds up so as to create a more serious affliction that requires medical attention, it is still in our best interest to revisit the source of the stagnant energy and release what remains through forgiveness and release.

This practice is a work in progress, but I am experiencing it firsthand both in real time and retroactively, and I have found that I have been able to wean myself off of the prescribed medication for both my thyroid and my Rheumatoid Arthritis and am now officially medicine free for the first time since 1996!

My take away: Let go of the **fear of the shame** because NOTHING feels better than the freedom experienced on the other side.

Ninth Recommandment

I shalt not become so myopic
in my perspective of what IS
that I can no longer see
beyond the discomfort in which
I presently reside.

Rather, I SHALL recognize that everything is connected, and although isolated events and experiences may be seemingly unrelated, often upon further inspection, all roads lead to the same thing—my personal growth, my personal empowerment, and my feelings of joy, peace, and freedom.

This understanding leads me to the understanding that my perspective is my reality, and if I shift my perspective, I shift my reality, transmuting all circumstances through my thoughts, then beliefs, then actions.

When people visit Ubuntu Fish Gallery, I am always delighted to share the story of how I got here. I tell them how I was a career educator, who by happenstance picked up a paint brush in 2015 and discovered my bliss. I proudly share how I courageously followed my true calling, and within two years, I had left my job, sold my house, gave up my frivolous lifestyle, painted in the woods for two years, and yadda, yadda, yadda, here I stand in this beautiful gallery, living this beautiful life of purpose, peace, and freedom. I wrap my story in a beautiful bow and gift it to anybody who will listen, but I will share with you the back story.

I mentioned in *Attachment to Career Identity* that the perfect storm of circumstances became the catalyst for my leaving YHS, but I remember vividly the moment my decision was made.

The foundation of my entire educational career was based on the pattern of *life is hard; I must fight to overcome the obstacles*, which presented itself in my constant fight for what I believed to be right to meet the needs of the children, when truly, my constant fight for what I believed to be right was to meet the needs of the child I once was. On some level, I believed I was being the adult that I needed, and I was righting all of the wrongs of the misinformed adults that I had experienced in my life. On some level, I was. However, at the time, I did not understand that although we think we are on quests to help others, we are always first and foremost on our own quest for personal growth and expansion. *Save the children:* this is what drove me; this is where I thrived.

About seven years into my career, when I began working at YHS, I continued the pattern of championing for what I believed was in the best interest of the children, often pushing against the grain to do so. My job was sometimes frustrating and often exhausting, but it totally aligned with my belief systems at the time and was incredibly rewarding.

As the school evolved, and the students and faculty expanded, both populations became incredibly heterogenous, but the school, which began as a very small and homogenous community, didn't accommodate for that expansion, creating even more frustration and exhaustion, especially around the areas of special needs and behavioral modification, which were both in my wheelhouse. At YHS, I wore many, many hats, but special-ed and behavior mod were my primary focus and my home run swing.

As we evolve as human beings, our emotional guidance systems offer us opportunities to decide what we don't like. We then can move in the direction of what we do like, and our experiences can offer us opportunities to learn lessons for our personal expansion. Lessons gone unlearned become more challenging until they become uncomfortable. Then, they eventually become unbearable until the lesson is learned and the expansion is complete. As you already know, however, when we ignore the lesson and get stuck in the emotionality and get lost in the victim/victor pattern, we ultimately get punched in the you know what. YOU know what!

In the last few years of my tenure at YHS, the population had tripled, the number of students with special academic and behavioral needs grew exponentially, and the program that I had developed over a decade prior had not grown in tandem with the population. I put up the good fight. I had adjusted and amended and thrown on as many band aids as I was able, but as much as I fought for what I thought was right and just, I was left feeling disempowered, frustrated, and mostly angry.

What I didn't understand was that I was given opportunity after opportunity after opportunity over those last few years to evolve out of my unhealthy belief systems that no longer served me. Instead, I became entrenched in my emotions, attached to my beliefs and my identity, and dug in my heels, put on my gloves, and continued to fight the good fight.

During this time, I was gifted a carrot or two or three to ease the process of letting go. I discovered an ability to create art, an ability that had lain dormant in me for three decades. I was gifted this beautiful new family, which was the only thing that I ever really wanted. In 2015, I was gifted Rheumatoid Arthritis, a severe physical affliction that was exacerbated by stress in order to help me gauge how much stress I was experiencing. Carrots everywhere, but I was so myopic about what I believed was right and just that I was unable to see the big picture and only focused on what I wanted in that moment—*the children's needs aren't being met, Dana's needs aren't being met*—I could see nothing else.

I was miserable at my job. I was miserable in my body, and the situation was getting progressively worse. I had a few students in my classroom that were, through no fault of their own, misplaced in the system, and because their needs weren't being met, not only were they NOT thriving, but they were also failing miserably and getting into behavioral trouble at every turn. Because my career identity was involved, having them in two classes, creating academic and behavioral plans for the other teachers for them, and handling disciplinary action with them on a systemic level, the fight became personal; not to mention, this was a private school and money and politics often trumped what I felt was right and just, only fueling my completely irrational belief systems and attachment to identity. To throw in just another punch to the old you know what, the level of support from the powers that be was not only nonexistent, but it was also undermining, which fed into my need for abandonment.

By April 2016, I was stuck and looking for no solutions other than to feel anger and resentment. Then this happened. A colleague and friend of mine brought two of the usual suspects to my office for a disciplinary visit. It was Groundhog Day. Same students. Same story. Same tied hands. After I gave them the same diatribe and the same consequence and the same level of disappointment, I heard the following conversation in my head:

"Blah, blah, blah...You two need to get your heads out of your asses!"

To which I responded to myself, "You can't say that to fifteen-year-old boys."

Then I paused, metaphorically punched myself in the twat, and said out loud, "You both need to get your heads out of your asses and get your acts together."

I then dismissed them from my office; I looked at Tom, my coworker, and knew my time was up at YHS. In that moment, on some level, under different circumstances, maybe, I would have received a phone call from a parent or maybe my principal would have slapped me on the wrist, but I knew.

Even Tom told me later that he had seen me in action

many times. We worked together for many years, but he had never seen that look on my face. He said he could only describe it as resolve or even resignation. Again, none of it was consciously intentional, but on some level that I am still not sure I understand, I knew that a shit storm was on the horizon.

Like I expected, the boys told their parents and our head of school about my *head in the ass* comment, knowing it might reduce the temperature of their hot water a bit. Their parents and our head of school responded in kind because knocking me off my pedestal might slow my roll a little bit.

What I hadn't expected, however, was that everything—my beliefs, my purpose, my identity, my reputation, my patterns, everything—would be called into question with this one sentence—*Get your heads out of your asses.*

Nobody had my back! My colleagues had their opinions, but they had to protect their interests. My head of school threw me under the bus, ran me over, then backed up and ran me over again, but he had to protect his interests. My feelings of loss, victimization and abandonment were indescribable. I was in fetal position for weeks over this because I knew it was time to go, but concurrently, my husband happened to get laid off during this time, and I convinced myself that I needed the income, and I wasn't ready to give up my "stability" because evidently, financial stability beats physical and emotional health and wellness when you're playing the game of life, or at least that was my belief at the time. It was a true disaster. I was trapped by what I believed to be important, and I was broken by my attachment to all of it. Truly heartbroken, I completed the school year at the end of May and returned on August 1st with my resignation in hand.

The whole experience was just so painful, and if I am being honest with myself, my understanding of having created this experience came sometime after. I suffered greatly while contemplating this "loss", observing it from every angle and seeing it from different perspectives. The one constant, though, was my inability to see myself as anything but the victim, and THAT is what was keeping me stuck. Even my initial drive to succeed with my art career was fueled by the bitterness of being able to say "I told you so!"

I grieved hard for a year as I shed both my pain and attachments a little at a time, and with the shedding of each layer, I received a little more clarity, and with each new layer of clarity, I discovered a new layer of compassion and a new layer of forgiveness—at first for all the players that *let me down* but ultimately for myself for not understanding how this all works—for not understanding that my beliefs create my experiences, for just not knowing. What I also learned was that processing these painful experiences takes time. My understanding of my experience at YHS did not come as an AH-HA moment, rather it came in waves, waves of understanding, one wave at a time—first as a realization, then came my willingness to look at it, then my willingness to perceive it in a different way, then my willingness to be gentle and not all judgey with myself, then my willingness to forgive myself, and THEN came my willingness to let it all go.

Then something really cool happens. Another realization comes and you go through this process again, and it becomes less shameful. Then another realization comes, and this process gets even easier, and then you begin to apply it to other aspects of your life. Then you develop real compassion for yourself, like true self-acceptance and self-love, and when that happens, you begin to feel compassion for others, and your life becomes more peaceful, and you develop more clarity and you *truly* are free.

The reality is that the fear of seeing ourselves and feeling the deeply embedded shame that we carry is what's holding us from freedom, but when we commit to ourselves and become honest with ourselves and look at ourselves and love ourselves, we begin to understand that nothing is more fear inducing than living under that veil of fear. Nothing is more fear-inducing than attaching to a safety net filled with obsolete beliefs, patterns, and paradigms that are no longer serving us. Nothing.

The expression *It's always darkest before the dawn* is quite cliché, but like all cliches, it's seeded in the truth. If we can detach ourselves from the emotion of the unpleasant experience, sometimes just for a moment, we can gain just a little more clarity. Although it's difficult to see how the parts affect the whole, if we can learn to trust that all roads lead to the same thing—my personal growth, my personal empowerment, and my feelings of joy, peace, and freedom—we can learn to extract the opportunities with lesser pain, fewer punches, and with a broader perspective of the world in which we live.

It is important to note that although every day is an opportunity to learn, grow, and expand, this was the last of my real emotionally traumatic experiences to date, because as we become adept at identifying the beliefs and behaviors that keep us stuck, the lessons become easier, more streamlined, and become more of a tickle of a feather than a punch to the, well, you know...

Tenth Recommandment

I shalt not live in fear.

Rather, I shall recognize that all thoughts, emotions, and behaviors reside in just two camps: Love and Fear. Period. This awareness helps me recognize my own thought and behavioral patterns and affords me regular opportunities to alter my state of being by shifting to love every time I find myself in fear.

At this point, I have presented irrational belief systems in a variety of different ways and discussed them ad nauseum, but by this point, my hope is that you recognize that everything, I mean EVERYTHING that you experience and how you experience it is rooted in your beliefs. The healthier and more balanced the beliefs, the healthier and more balanced the experiences; the healthier and more balanced the experiences, the healthier and more balanced the life. It's truly that simple. When thoughts, experiences, and lives are unhealthy and imbalanced, it is because they are unequivocally rooted in fear.

When babies are born, other than their basic needs for comfort, safety, and security, they are literally the Tabula Rasa of love, absorbing all that is imbued within them.

They are essentially adorable little love sponges that require nothing but their needs being met for survival.

As related in the Fourth Recommandment—fear begins to emerge very early on when the child's most basic needs aren't being met, causing them to feel unsafe and insecure. Otherwise, children are overflowing with love and wonder and overall yumminess.

The only logical conclusion is that children are taught fear. With every opportunity to feel vulnerable, another lesson in fear is learned. As the child progresses, and their psychology becomes more complex, the degrees of fear and the ways in which the fear is expressed become more complex and varied.

Like everything else, nothing is ever just one thing. When considering love and fear, there is of course a spectrum based on the intensity of the emotion. Imagine a straight line. To the far left is fear and to the far right sits love. Every other emotion in varying degrees of intensity falls somewhere on that line, residing in one camp or another.

Emotions, such as anger, frustration, anxiety, overwhelm, irritation, sadness, disgust, envy, guilt, shame, hostility are all based in fear. Emotions, such as happiness, gratitude, pleasure, contentment, peace, joy, hope, and faith are all based in love. Simply put, when you are feeling an unpleasant emotion, it is based in fear, and when you are feeling a pleasant emotion, it is based in love.

I am not suggesting that fear be eradicated completely. Fear-based emotions have their place in our existence because they alert us to danger, challenging situations, and experiences that are unpleasant for us. Fear does have its role as a part of our emotional guidance system, but otherwise, fear is unhealthy and superfluous and is often used as a means of manipulation or control.

Love also has a role in our emotional guidance system, but truly love is the essence of all things and our most natural state of being. We all, every single one of us, are born into this world as a concentrated, tiny bundle of love. Our interpretation and integration of our experiences and the unresolved emotions that we attach to them are what then dictate our personal trajectories after that.

How do we release the fear?

How do you eat an elephant? One piece at a time!

Unfortunately, fear is ubiquitous in our culture and has come to be completely accepted and normalized by the masses. Fear appears in many forms of entertainment, sports, television programs, Hollywood movies, advertisements, social media accounts, politics, the news, business, relationships, families, medical institutions, educational systems, religion, mythology—it is everywhere!

Because each one of us carries fear in one form or another based on our own personal imbalances, we resonate with our fear driven society, and frankly, we do not give it much thought. However, if you accept the truths of ANY of the previous recommmandments, then you understand that in order to be *fear-less*, you must become personally empowered. Nothing externally matters nor will it change until you create the changes within yourself. Period.

1. Create more awareness of yourself, what drives you, and if you are not driven by a loving force, investigate why.

2. It's always best to begin addressing your fear at the source of your fear-based beliefs, but be gentle and kind to yourself and begin where you are able—*one piece at a time.*

3. Focus on YOUR fear-based beliefs only. We all empower ourselves at our own pace and trying to push others along is A. based in fear and B. fear inducing in and of itself.

Our truest essence is love, and if you've found yourself a little left of center on that spectrum, remember love in all of its forms has not been lost on you. It is for you to look within, do the work, and release that which sullies your essence, *one piece at a time.*

Trust the Process

Trusting the process can be difficult because we are inundated with billions of opinions on how the process *should* look. In the process of rediscovering ourselves, our true selves, often the first thing we do is look to someone or something else to figure out what that is. We watch videos, read books, regurgitate memes, adopt rituals and practices, and sift through a plethora of different "how-to" guides in order to find ourselves. However, the reality is nobody knows you better than you. You know what feels good. You know what doesn't feel good.

Hot tip: Do more things that feel good!

The key is to remember the momentum that landed you in this place, right here, right now. Reversing that momentum begins as a step-by-step process, beginning right here, right now.

Sometimes, the process feels like it doesn't make any sense and the actions that you take to create contentment for yourself in this moment are seemingly unrelated to where you eventually want to be, but it's as simple as, if it feels good, do it, asking yourself, "What can I do in this moment, right here, right now, to become one step closer to contentment?"

Remember, anything that you do that's for your greater good begins with this moment, THIS moment, and also remember, "you've gotta have faith, faith, faith."

Faith

Faith is a tricky word. For me two things would come to mind when I would hear the word faith: George Michael and religion. The former makes me smile but the latter, I must admit, would make my back go up a bit. Because I consider myself a tolerant and open-minded person, I feel I must explore this visceral reaction to the word faith. Here is what I uncovered.

What people sometimes don't realize is that faith is just trust in a belief that we hold. Because the vast majority of us, through our personal experiences, have lost the ability to trust our own beliefs because they were built on a foundation of fear and mistrust, we have stopped relying on our own emotional guidance systems, healthy belief systems, physical guidance systems, balanced chakra systems, essentially all of our own inherent personal systems of empowerment that have become misaligned and dysfunctional from years of abuse and neglect. We have become distrustful of our OWN ability to create a life that brings us joy and contentment. We've lost faith in ourselves, often leaving us lost and vulnerable and searching outwardly for something to rely on, something to have faith in.

By searching outwardly, we set ourselves up for disappointment and disempowerment. We have put our own contentment in the hands of others—in the hands of our loved ones, our jobs, our culture, our religious leaders, our politicians, our parents, our children; the list goes on.

Having faith in ideas, people, and institutions outside of yourself, however, is by no means a crime. Quite the contrary, it is quite beautiful to live in a state of openness and trust and to have faith in the world around you, but to solely trust what's outside of you can be detrimental to your personal empowerment because your contentment is always at the mercy of another.

Through this paradigm, we learn to placate ourselves with mantras like *I guess it was supposed to be that way* or *everything happens for a reason,* which only masks our disappointment and fuels our disempowerment. So, what's the answer?

Trust the Purpose

Often people of faith share the mindset of *everything happens for a reason.* I was always turned off by this notion, and I remember in my twenties grappling with the contradiction of, *does everything happen for a reason? Or as intelligent thinking beings, do we just attach a reason to experiences so as to cope with the unpleasant ones with a little more ease?*

Now at fifty, I understand that neither is true. All experiences are experiences. They are just information that leads us to the next experience. It is our judgement of the experience and our unresolved emotional response to that experience that results in our emotional attachment to it, and in many cases, it keeps us stuck there without having learned much from it.

What I've come to realize is that my distaste for *everything happens for a reason* is mostly because that phrase is just another way to release personal power from the experiences that we have. Instead, everything that happens is a result of a cause-and-effect relationship, and our reaction to these cause-and-effect relationships comes with purpose: the purpose of personal expansion.

The purpose is to either alert us to what we don't want out of life, so we can begin to make strides toward what we do want or to teach us something about ourselves so that we can reflect on our own beliefs and patterns and reverse momentum of the beliefs and patterns that no longer serve us.

Sometimes the purpose isn't so cut and dry and some circumstances leave us feeling lost and broken and sometimes feeling hopeless. These circumstances are the most challenging because the intensity of the emotional toil is so powerful that it is easy to spin into the downward spiral of victimhood, begging the question *Why do these things always happen to me?* This questioning returns us to patterns that no longer serve us and the cycle continues.

The reality is, there is a reason. There is a purpose. There is a purpose to ALL of it. The purpose is to learn and grow and evolve as a human being and to the best of your ability to feel love and joy in doing so.

The purpose is up to you and your perspective. What

do YOU wish to gain? What do YOU want out of life? What can YOU gain from this shitty experience? Yes, everything does happen for a reason—something previously happened to cause it. Period. The purpose, however, is essentially whatever you choose to glean from the situation, aiding in your personal expansion.

If we respond with all of our tools of empowerment in a way that is in our own highest good and from an honest and well-balanced place, the purpose does not have to be obvious in the moment, for when hindsight offers an opportunity to observe through clearer eyes, the purpose is always revealed—and most often, the joy that is void in the more intense of learning opportunities begins to appear as the lessons become less challenging, and as we discover the joy as often as we can in as many opportunities as we can, we become rewarded with more opportunities to grow through more joyous experiences, and the purpose becomes clearer, and the joy becomes louder, and the momentum grows stronger, and your faith in the purpose becomes solid, and your appreciation for the process becomes heightened, and the fear just disappears. Oh my God! It's just so fucking beautiful!

By restoring balance and creating personal sovereignty with your sense of being, and by creating personal empowerment through reestablishing beliefs, patterns, and paradigms that you can trust, you begin to recognize the purpose and live more joyfully. You begin to create a faith in yourself, and by doing this, you create a clarity and broad view, expanding your internal faith externally, ultimately discovering that the peace and freedom that you desire is within your reach.

You come to realize that,

This is your life.

You have the power.

YOU choose.

And NOW you feel empowered to do so.

The End

Epilogue

I wrote this book because throughout my extensive and colorful life experiences, I've attained some sweet pearls of wisdom over the years.

I wrote this book because I truly believe that I have something valuable to share that could be beneficial to others in their own search for personal growth and empowerment.

What I didn't bank on was my own level of personal growth through the process of my writing.

The last few months have been so intense on both a physical and emotional level that, as I waded through past experiences that I had thought I had put to rest years ago, I had not anticipated that I would uncover layer after layer after layer of buried trauma that remained in my tissues and even on a deep cellular level.

I had not anticipated the amount of shame I have carried with me all of these years that was hidden so far beneath the surface completely unbeknownst to me! For my friends who know me well know that what you see is what you get with me. I am as happy and as well-adjusted as I portray, yet still I had no idea how much shame that I carried deep within me.

When I took the time, however, to poke around and reprocess my experiences from my healthy adult perspective, I was able to release the shame once and for all—truly a life changing experience.

The experience of writing this book was a great purge on so many levels. For me, it was more physical than emotional because that's where my shame was hidden, in my physicality. It hid in disease and physical maladies, and as I processed and conveyed my greatest hurts, I observed my body release in the process, sometimes laying me out for days at a time.

No joke, writing this book really kicked my ass!

I truly have no words for what this experience has gifted me—it has gifted me improved physical health, emotional wellness, and personal freedom.

My hope is that having read about these experiences and insights and perhaps gleaning some insights of your own, it has offered the same gifts to you.

Ubuntu!

Dana Sardano

is the owner, resident artist and intuitive at Ubuntu Fish Gallery in Stuart, Florida. She is also the Co-Founder, Chief Officer of Content + Curriculum, and Consigliere of FindUniquelyU.com, Co-Founder/Editor-in-Chief of Phenom Publishing, and Co-Host of *Cuddle Talk with Angela & Dana.*

Dana received her B.A. in Special Education in 1993,

specializing in Behavioral Disorders (BD) for children K-12. Her career path quickly shifted into a learning specialist position, which evolved into the position of director of student development in a private college preparatory high school, where she was hired as a teacher of humanities and where she assisted students with organizational skills and study strategies to help them better adapt in the mainstream classroom environment. Dana also spent the bulk of her career mentoring teachers and assisting them with their curriculum, content and instructional practices to better educate the whole child. For many years, creating specialized curriculum and behavioral modification plans for teachers was her jam! She learned very early on in her career that behavioral issues, academic achievement, and personal accountability for both went hand in hand (in hand), and built an entire career in mastering an understanding of how to impart this understanding to others.

After picking up a paintbrush for the first time in 2015 since her childhood, in June 2017, she decided to retire from a 23-year career in education in order to fully embrace an artist's life and to model for her daughters the importance of listening to your soul's purpose by following your bliss. She spent two years honing her craft as well as developing her intuition and opened Ubuntu Fish Gallery in September 2019, two years after she took her leap of faith from traditional education.

Experiencing for herself and offering for others a more creative and spiritual form of personal growth and development at Ubuntu Fish Gallery, Dana has never felt more alive and has made it her mission to help others do the same.

During Dana's time as owner/resident artist and intuitive at Ubuntu Fish Gallery, she figured out how to merge her greatest strengths—her intuition, leadership skills, educational experience, and artistic ability—and currently guides people to lead more empowered lives through her intuitive guidance sessions, private groups, and written works on that very subject matter.

Dana has also written and illustrated a book combined with a workbook for children called *Veda Finds Her Crown*, centered around chakra health and development to help aide teachers, parents, and caretakers who are educating the whole child. She has also followed up *Ten Recommandments for Personal Empowerment* with *Beyond the Ten, Decoding the Woo Woo,* an autobiographical account of her own spiritual journey, written with the hope of demystifying spiritual practices by presenting them in an understandable and practical way.

Dana's goal with all of her writing is to act as a bridge between the mainstream and the metaphysical communities so that those on the quest for personal growth and development can do so without being deterred by fearful and biased conceptions of spirituality. Her hope is to educate both the parents and the children so that they empower themselves and work together to create a new self-empowered, unity conscious generation.

Dana's role at Uniquely U. is to assist the like-minded U-Instructors of the Uniquely U. community so that they can embody *their* truest essence and galvanize themselves and others in a multitude of uplifting and self-empowering ways so that *they* can do the same for others.

For more information and to find Dana, visit:

- UbuntuFishGallery.com
- FindUniquelyU.com
- Phenom-Publishing.com

In Florida? Stop by Ubuntu Fish Gallery and say "Hello!" **Ubuntu Fish Gallery**, 508 SE Osceola St., Stuart, FL, 34994.

PUBLISHING

If you have passion in your heart and a voice for your spirit, then you should have the freedom to share it with others. When you uplift and inspire another through *your* stories of *your* greatness and *your* resilience then you are in your own right a phenom.

Phenom Publishing was created by Dana Sardano and Angela DiMarco for those of you who have something special to offer, something created from your soul and delivered through your heart, something that is yearning to be heard.

Phenom recognizes that within we are *all* phenoms, and through our creativity, we *all* have the ability to change our inner worlds which ultimately changes the world around us. Dana and Angela have begun by sharing their individual stories, and they encourage you to share yours so that humanity can unite and thrive in its phenomenal collective story.

If you have something to share and the voice to share it and are seeking a platform to share it on, join the movement and become the voice of the people.

Become a phenom.
Editors@Phenom-Publishing.com